D0193944

We're natural explorers. We're wanderers.

The only species out of 8.7 million species to completely surround the Earth. Every day we wake up and wonder, "where am I? Where am I going?"

Reinvention is in our genes. But often it's been repressed by institutions that want us standardized. Clones of each other so we can be easily replaced.

But...

Life is changing. The economy is changing. We are getting unstuck in our lives. The greatest opportunity we ever had to change and have the lives we want is happening right now.

Every time you reinvent, you need to figure out the variables for a simple equation:

PLUS: Who are the people you can learn from? Real mentors, virtual mentors.

EQUAL: Who are the people who can challenge us? We can't get better unless we are constantly challenged and then get feedback from our mentors.

MINUS: Who are the people we can teach and share with and make an impact on? Without this, one can never truly become a master.

The rest of this book will help you find your plus, minus, equal.

Reinvent YOURSELF

✦ ✦ ✦

JAMES ALTUCHER

COPYRIGHT © JAMES ALTUCHER, 2016. ALL RIGHTS RESERVED.

All rights reserved. No part of this publication may be reproduced, stored in or introduced into a retrieval system, or transmitted, in any form or by any means (electronically, mechanically, via photocopying, recording or otherwise), without the prior written permission of both the copyright owner and the publisher of this book. The scanning, uploading, and distribution of this book via the Internet or via any other means without the permission of the publisher is illegal and punishable by law.

Printed in the United States of America.

CATALOG:
ALTUCHER, JAMES
    Reinvent Yourself / James Altucher
p. cm.

First Edition
Interior designed by: Erin Tyler

CHOOSE YOURSELF
MEDIA LLC.

INTRODUCTION

I t was all over for me once again.

Marriage was over. My bank account going down. Nobody was publishing any more of my books. Nobody was giving me any more opportunities.

I'd wake up at 3 a.m. and I couldn't even breathe. I'd walk downstairs and start writing numbers down on pieces of paper. I'd add numbers together, subtract them, divide them. Whatever.

I couldn't add up to a number that would give me enough money to live.

Finally I took a job I couldn't stand. I hated the commute. I didn't get along with the people I worked with and I don't think they liked me very much.

On the second day on the job I fell down and hurt myself. I don't know why I fell. But by the time my train pulled into town, 70 miles north of N.Y.C. at that time, I was in so much pain I couldn't even walk. An older couple carried me off the train. It was embarrassing.

So I quit.

I started to day trade again. But that wasn't working. Some days I'd make a lot of money and other days I would lose. It was fine but I needed enough money to live and I couldn't figure out how to do it.

All these years I had built up my career. I had built and sold businesses. I had written books. I had run funds.

One day I simply couldn't take it anymore. I was alone. I was so scared I was shaking.

I decided to go swimming. I took a walk to a local beach. There was nobody there. I walked into the water. I went under the surface and thought maybe I could just float there forever. I felt like I didn't even need to breathe.

I swam until dark. Then I went home.

I sat down and wrote about everything going wrong in my life. I was unhappy with my career. I felt like I should be doing something I loved every day.

I was unhappy with my relationships. I didn't seem to have many friends.

All my life, I had tried to be creative, but I kept trying to force that creativity into something that would generate money instead of just being creative just for the sake of it.

And, as I was writing things down, I realized I had forgotten to be grateful for the good things in my life. It was as if my brain had been exiled from all the wonderful things that had happened to me to make me who I was.

From that day I started to change.

I realized that I was an amateur. I had spent my life pretending to be something I wasn't.

I wanted to move beyond to that.

....

TO:

....

* Have humility. Learn from everyone you can. Even if it's just one takeaway.
* Be grateful for the many lessons you get, and realize that everything is a lesson.
* Only be around people you love and who inspire you.
* Life is a billion times smaller than the point of a needle. Don't waste it doing things you were told to do. Do the things you love to do.
* Health is the most important thing, else your body today won't let you enjoy tomorrow.
* Every day, be creative. Creativity is a muscle.
* You're going to make mistakes, but 80% is always good enough. Keep learning the next thing.
* Life will constantly hit you until you are senseless. Don't forget these are lessons.

And finally, the amateur learns to laugh every day. That's when he turns pro.

Children laugh an average of 300 times a day. Adults on average...five times a day.

What else is there?

TABLE OF CONTENTS

IT'S GOING TO BE A
STORM! DO YOU HAVE
AN UMBRELLA?

H ere's how things will go bad. And it will happen.

Incomes are getting lower every year. This will never stop.

Since 1993, income for people age 18-35 has gone from $36,000 to $33,000.

This seems like a small amount.

It's not. It's the first time ever that income has gone down over such a long period (more than a year).

This means: relying on college, a job, promotions, security, stability, pension, retirement income = thing of the past.

That reliability doesn't exist anymore.

Meanwhile debt has gone straight up. Student loan debt, credit card debt, housing debt.

Of course a key to survival that I've written about many times is: don't buy a house, don't go to college, and either don't get credit cards or stop paying back your debt (I won't argue the ethics—they are there. If you meet me in a back alley with a lead pipe we can either fight to the death or we can discuss the ethics of not paying back credit card debt.)

But there's a more serious problem:

A) DEMAND HAS GONE DOWN.

Because of outsourcing and automation, the basic equation of all economics throughout history has been reversed.

Supply is almost infinite (it costs nothing now to make an iPhone in China.)

Demand has gone down. (Because everything is cheaper, you don't need to spend as much money. Also, computers are basically "finished"—you don't need any more features. I haven't upgraded a computer or a phone in years. And that's just one thing. All across the board, I don't need to upgrade or spend more. If the bookstore raises prices, all the more reason for me to buy e-books.)

B) THE RICH ARE GETTING RICHER.

There are three reasons for this:

1) *The bailouts saved the economy. But at a cost.*

I won't get into the technical details. What for? But in 2009, the U.S. Central Bank printed up a few extra trillion dollars.

The theory is that that money would be spread throughout the economy. Poor and rich.

That's not what happened. Banks got bailed out. Bonuses went up. And a rich person puts the extra dollar in the bank while a poor person pays the rent.

So the money went into the banks, which no longer lend out money to poor people because the Central Bank keeps giving them money.

2) *Some of the extra money went to infrastructure projects that the government did.*

This is good.

Doing research to increase the supply of food and the supply of technology is great. But see above: increases in supply without increases in demand = deflation, fewer jobs, lower income.

3) *Intergenerational robbing of the poor.*

I sat on a plane next to a high-ranking former government official.

He no longer works for the government. Instead, other governments hire him to help them figure out how to control their citizens so that they can stay in power.

OK, I didn't judge him. I just wanted to know what he knew.

He showed me. He pulled out chart after chart. He said they had studied this for many years.

"Look."

And here is what he basically spent four hours telling me (we were sitting next to each other on a red-eye from LA).

By the way, he was unhealthy, overweight, and drinking the entire time. But he kept pulling reports out of his briefcase, compiled by people who work for him.

"I'm scared for the future. Terrified really."

Basically, rich people send their kids to "Harvard" (I put it in quotes because substitute your high-priced, elite college of choice).

Harvard boys meet Harvard girls. They get married. They get great jobs. They make a lot of money.

They have kids and their kids go to Harvard and meet other Harvard kids and make even more money.

So, in addition to the bailouts and other government incentives, culturally we are in a society where, across generations, the rich only get richer.

Poor people have the reverse equation. They keep meeting other poor people, having children with them who are even poorer, and those kids marry poor people.

This is overly simplistic. But this is what he was showing me.

The generations of increasing poor (or lower class, since "poor" is not a number but is now basically an inequality, something relative to the highest class) want someone extreme. Someone who will go into bank accounts and transfer money from rich to poor.

He said, "Trump and Sanders both appeal to that. That's why ex-Sanders supporters don't even like Hillary."

It's not Democrat versus Republican anymore. Trump is not

even a Republican. And Sanders wasn't a Democrat.

It's the small rich at the top of the pyramid and the huge masses of poor at the bottom, and they will eventually win.

* * *

THIS IS NOT A BOOK ABOUT ECONOMICS.

Or about government. Or revolution.

This is about what you should be doing in your living room right now. This is about how you and your family can survive.

This is about how you can flourish and be in a constant state of reinvention.

A) YOU CAN'T RELY ON GOVERNMENT OR EDUCATIONAL INSTITUTIONS.

They are primarily designed to make the rich richer and the poor poorer.

I do not say this in a political way. I have ZERO interest in political issues. This is simply what is happening. This is what the data is showing. This is what I am seeing from my hedge fund friends every day.

This is reality.

They will want you to succumb to their pressures:

Go to school and get into debt with the government with no guarantee of a job.

Borrow money from the banks that got their money from the central bank so you can buy a house whose price will no longer go up.

Take a job working for the rich shareholders of massive corporations so you can get paid less while increasing supply for the few who can have access to expensive cancer drugs, driverless cars, robots, etc.

B) CHOOSE YOURSELF.

Which of course I write about a lot. BUT...

Take it a step further.

I always say it first has to come from within: physical, emotional, mental, and spiritual health. I.e., write down 10 ideas a day. Be around good people. Be grateful, etc.

But you also have to look at an important data point: the IRS says the average multi-millionaire has seven different sources of income.

When you have one source of income—for instance, a job—you are falling into the trap. You will be one of the masses instead of one of the people who will survive. So you constantly have to be on the lookout for the other sources of income I write about repeatedly.

C) REINVENT YOURSELF

The world is changing quickly. A few years ago we didn't have tablets or smartphones. Now a billion+ people have them.

A few decades ago we didn't have search engines. Now everyone has all the knowledge in the world at their fingertips.

The greatest artists (Picasso is a good example) reinvented themselves every five years.

The best businesspeople (Steve Jobs, Elon Musk and Richard Branson are all great examples) reinvented themselves every few years.

Five years and you need to start learning new skills, practicing new efforts, trying on new careers for size.

All the people I've ever had on my podcast—200 successful artists, billionaires, astronauts, athletes, writers, entrepreneurs, inventors—have reinvented themselves over and over.

D) WELL-BEING

What is reinvention?

Finding new sources of income. We can't ignore that money is important. Money buys freedom.

Finding well-being. When I was in my 20s I had no idea what well-being meant. I thought "happiness" meant a private plane, a big house, fame, whatever.

As the director Tom Shadyac (who gave all his millions and moved into a trailer park) told me:

"Happiness is based on the world 'happenstance,' which refers to something outside of yourself."

You need to find well-being from within.

And here is what it is:

FREEDOM

RELATIONSHIPS

COMPETENCE

Increase those every day and you will find well-being.

If all you do is the same thing every day, you will never increase those three things in your life.

So reinvention occurs every day. It's not something you wake up every five years and say, "OK, today is Reinvention Day."

So reinvention is:

* Defining freedom in different ways (reducing expectations, increasing sources of income so no one source controls you).
* Improving relationships. Plus, minus, equal: Finding mentors to teach you. Finding the next generation to teach. Finding friends who build you up and challenge you. This is your "scene." Everyone going through reinvention needs a scene.

* Habits. It's the 5x5 rule. You are not just the average of the five people around you. You're the average of the five habits you do, the things you eat, the ideas you have, the content you consume, etc.

* * *

IT'S TOO LATE.

Do you know what an event horizon is?

It's the area around a black hole where gravity is stronger than anything. Once you are beyond the event horizon, nothing can prevent you from going into the center of the black hole.

You are swallowed up.

It's the point of being "too late."

Society is crossing the event horizon. The black hole is the coming war of "Us vs. Them." This war will be fought in elections, in your bank accounts, in your career, in your relationships, in the streets.

It will rip apart everything we know.

But by reinventing yourself you can avoid it.

I am an optimist. It might not seem like that because of what I've written above. But I am hopeful that I will survive. I have been through every failure imaginable. Loss of family. Loss of health. Loss of mind. Loss of money.

I've applied these techniques to my own life. Over the past 10 years, I've seen others apply them.

And in the past three years I've interviewed hundreds of other people who are aware of what is happening.

They have reinvented themselves. They have thrived. They have surfed the rage that is simmering underneath and ridden that rage to greater highs and greater hopes.

These people will save the world. They are not the 1%. They are outside of the category, in my opinion.

You and I can be like these people. They have all started where we start. They have done it and made it to the finish line and beyond.

This is now the time to do it. It's going to be too late tomorrow. And it was too early yesterday.

Today reinvention begins.

THE ULTIMATE GUIDE TO FINDING A MENTOR

For better or for worse, I have reinvented many times over the past 30 years. I used to be worried that I was reinventing TOO MANY times.

Why, every other year or so, I find myself stuck or frustrated and needing to take the next step forward or face misery?

But the reality is: reinvention is life. This is the call to adventure that constantly whispers to us. Do we answer it? Do we take the call?

After my dad went into a permanent coma I had to take his car back to the dealership and hand them the keys. They wanted to know what happened and I couldn't talk. I couldn't sign papers. I was shaking.

I held out the keys and they took them. I walked out. My dad was my first mentor.

Afterward, I was waiting on the curb of the highway for a car to pick me up. I got a message:

"Come to dinner."

So of course I dropped all my plans and went. It was from someone who was mentoring me.

Much later that night I had too much to drink. At my instigation, the mentor's daughter (who I had a crush on, and who's now a well-known movie producer) screamed at the mentor's mistress ("Money-hungry slut!") and then walked out of The Four Seasons restaurant.

Mentorship over. But there are many ways to find a PLUS in your life. Both real and virtual.

I've had about eight or nine mentors in my life. I've had many more virtual mentors. And it's an ongoing process. I try to learn from everyone. I constantly try to find people I respect who can teach me what they do. Right now I have mentors ranging in age from 20 to 80.

I also get better at the quality of people who mentor me. No more mistresses, for instance. But this was a learning process.

Learning never stops. Many people die at 25 but are not put in the coffin until 75. The learning stopped for them early.

Every day I seek out mentors: people who have great experience to help me, particularly in areas I am new to, excited about, and know nothing about.

Here are the only ways I've ever been able to find a mentor. I hope they work for you as well.

A) RESEARCH

I do heavy research on their bios, their histories, everything. One time I even read an academic paper written in 1965 by one person who I wanted to mentor me and I sent him my comments on it.

I read all the books they like and have spoken publicly about. I read all the analysis on the books so I can discuss it with them. I read all of their books. I read about people they've previously mentored and what happened.

This may seem overly coordinated or manipulative. But this is the real world and not the land of legend where magical caddies help golf pros deal with a spiritual crisis in the middle of the most important tournament of their lives.

B) VALUE

I send ideas for how they can improve their businesses. I still do this every day. I just did it about 20 minutes ago with a business I want to learn more about.

But this involves even more work and research. For me at least, I have to put in a lot of time before someone wants to spend time with me.

The ideas have to be so good that it's possible they have never thought of them before. I write, let it sit, rewrite, let other people look at them sometimes, and finally send.

C) QUANTITY

Some people are simply too busy and will never be a mentor. They already have their mentees. Or they just don't want to. That's fine.

But, that said, I have a technique here, which is to provide updates every three to four months. This has worked for me in about two or three cases where they have eventually gotten back in touch. One of those cases resulted in the sale of a company I started.

Also, quantity is important because there is never just one thing you have been placed on this Earth to do. Life is a buffet and not a fixed-price meal. Speaking for myself, I like to sample.

D) AVAILABILITY

Even if they like your ideas and they send a friendly note back, there is still work to do.

I might fly out (even to another country where they might be) and then tell them, "I'm in the neighborhood, happy to discuss the ideas more."

I make myself available for whenever they are available because, by definition, they are less available than I am.

I am not available 99.9% of the time. But I always make myself available for people who I look up to as mentors.

I'm infinitely grateful for these people who have spent some of their hard-earned time on me. Every day I wake up grateful for that.

E) DIVERSITY

There's never just one mentor who will teach you "the ropes." I've always been on the lookout for more than one, usually at the same time.

It's also not a love relationship. I definitely am willing to "trade up" when I have a mentor.

If he or she is a good mentor, then this is something they would want for me. Many mentors fail in this respect. One of my first realizations was that mentors are never as perfect as I initially think they are.

F) VIRTUAL

Believe it or not, sometimes it's just as good (often better) to read all of their materials rather than be directly mentored.

Some people are very smart and you can get a lot of value from them but they are very draining when they are in person. I don't know why this is. Some people suck all of the air out of a room and they don't realize it about themselves.

One mentor I was over the moon about, but I found that whenever I was around him personally I would end up feeling bad about myself.

So there are different levels of engagement: reading, sending emails, taking courses, meeting in person, meeting in person every day.

Make sure you choose the right one that doesn't drain you.

But all of these methods of receiving the message of mentorship are equally viable depending on the mentor and what you want from them.

G) DELIVER

It's not just ideas. Sometimes I've wanted someone to mentor me (or notice me) and they aren't interested in ideas. So I will drive business their way, or introduce them to people who can provide value for them, etc.

This might be every three or four months. Just seeds I keep planting.

But it shows that I'm the type of person who can deliver, even if it's just the first review on their latest book. Something little every three or four months. This has helped me considerably (another company sold, for instance, after seven years of doing this without expectation).

H) OVER-DELIVER

This is your only chance. And your mentor has plenty of people around him. Over-deliver on everything. Look for every opportunity to over-deliver.

I) MICRO-MENTORSHIP

To this day, I have many mentors that I turn to for their areas of expertise even if it's not a main area of exploration in my life.

It's OK for someone to be a mentor for a day. Napoleon Hill interviewed Andrew Carnegie for one day and after that considered Carnegie a mentor for life. The mentor that ultimately influenced one of the top-selling books of the past 100 years: "Think and Grow Rich."

J) TIME

The best mentorships I've had have taken a lot of time to cement.

I provide a little value, they ask for more, I provide more value, we meet, they ask for more, I provide more value, they critique, we lose touch, I later provide more value, we spend more time together (then the mentoring occurs), I provide more value, they provide value for me (finally…payback), I provide more value, we trade value, I move on, then they hate me (90% of the time).

Why do they hate me? A poor mentor can't handle when the student goes sideways or higher. A good mentor will, with his last breath, push you to the top of the mountain, even at their own personal risk.

Most mentors lean toward "poor" in this regard, but a few are in the middle. And "good" is rare. At some point you will be a mentor. Please, please, listen to me and be a good mentor.

Your legacy is not what you do. It's what the people who you teach do.

Which leads me to…

I'm very grateful that in the past 20 years I've had many opportunities to be a mentor. It hasn't always been me on the floor crying. Sometimes I've done well and have been able to share.

When I'm the mentor: someone provides immense value for me, I show how the value could've been done better, and that cycle continues until they either surpass me (happens a lot, which is always my hope for the mentee) or they stop delivering value. Or they never fully delivered value in the first place and it took me awhile to realize.

The benefit they get is my comments on how they can provide more value to people and that might include introductions, advising their companies, suggestions, hiring, etc.

If they stop providing value, that's OK also. People's lives go in different directions and only sometimes do we intersect.

But I'm patient and many people come back, often years later and in much different capacities. This is happening to me now in at least two situations that are very important to me.

I always want people to succeed past me. What I usually say is, "When you later see me lying in a puddle of my urine in the gutter with a needle coming out of my eyeball, please pull me out so I don't get wet."

They laugh.

"That will never happen."

But deep down, I'm afraid it might come true.

HOW TO HAVE
1,000 MENTORS IN
YOUR LIFE

I wake up many mornings totally lost. Like every day. "Where am I?" For the smallest of seconds, I'm a stranger in my own body. In my own life.

And then the whole history of life swoops down and I'm like, "Ugh!"

The daily search for answers starts. Never-ending. Will someone tell me something new?

*　*　*

I WANTED PRAKASH TO BE MY MENTOR.

So I went and offered to take his class notes and turn them into a book. After that I spent time with him every day for months.

I wanted Victor be to my mentor. So I sent him free software for his trading. I sent him everything I had ever worked on. I read every book he ever quoted from. I read papers he wrote in the 1960s and referred to them.

He started me in my hedge fund business.

I wanted Jim to be my mentor. So I read all of his articles and I wrote to him: "Here are 10 articles I wish you would write."

And then he said, "How about you write them?"

And I wrote for him for years until he bought a company I started. I still look for mentors every day.

✦ ✳ ✦

MAYBE THEY WROTE SOMETHING THAT DROVE ME CRAZY WITH DELIGHT.

That solved problems in my life. Or maybe they created something beautiful. So I wanted to know how they did it.

Susan Cain wrote the book *Quiet* about unlocking the power of introverts. Her book has been on the bestseller list for the past three years.

Sometimes when I'm in a meeting or at a dinner, everyone is laughing and talking but I feel a shadow come up inside of me. It starts in my stomach, where the butterflies are.

It then crawls through my heart, gripping it, whispering, "Shhhh..." when the heart protests.

It climbs through my neck, freezing the muscles in my jaw and eventually clamps over my head.

And that's it. I'm done. I can't talk for the rest of the night.

So I called Susan Cain. It took months to figure out how to get through.

But I kept pursuing. Finally she came on my podcast. She has a great new company at QuietRev.com where she helps companies bring out the power of their introverted employees.

I wanted to talk about that.

But what I really wanted to talk about was what to do when I freeze up like that at an important dinner and meeting.

She gave me a bunch of suggestions. She said, "You need to be by yourself. So excuse yourself for a little bit when you get that feeling and recharge."

She said, "Listen to music or comedy beforehand." (Yay!)

She said, "Establish deadlines in advance so everyone knows that you are planning on leaving early."

She said, "Strike up one-on-one bonding with the people around you rather than trying to impress the whole group."

She said, "Be the first to arrive. So you can claim some mental ownership of the space."

She said many other things. The entire podcast was, of course, a therapy session for me. I hope she got her objectives as well out of the podcast. I highly recommend her book.

I highly recommend everything she says.

THE TAKEAWAY

Everything I do, everyone I meet, I try to find at least one take-away. THE PLUS.

Then I write it down. I try to remember everything. I talk to my friends about the takeaway. THE EQUAL

I share the takeaway. With the MINUS, I try to solidify what I've learned from everyone I meet.

My two themes:

* At the end of the day have I done my own daily practice. Without following my own advice, the advice becomes worthless.
* And have I continued to develop my PLUS, MINUS, EQUALS. They compound exponentially into an exponential life.

....

THE CONCEPT OF "PLUS, MINUS, EQUAL" COMES FROM THE GREAT MIXED MARTIAL ARTS FIGHTER AND INSTRUCTOR, FRANK SHAMROCK, WHOSE APPROACH WAS BROUGHT TO MY ATTENTION BY RYAN HOLIDAY IN HIS EXCELLENT BOOK, *EGO IS THE ENEMY*.

....

7

THE SEVEN TECHNIQUES TO INFLUENCE ANYONE

I f I could tell my children to read one chapter of this book, it would be this chapter.

Influence is how they will navigate a world of uncertainty.

Robert Cialdini is the most influential person in the world. And by that I mean, he wrote the book "Influence," which sold three million copies and defines the six critical aspects of all influence.

Now he has a new book, "Pre-Suasion," which goes 10 times deeper into the concepts of persuasion. I got him on my podcast so I could ask the 1,000 questions I have.

Small random facts from the book: If you name a restaurant "Studio 97" instead of "Studio 17," people are more likely to tip higher.

Another fact: If you ask a girl for her phone number outside a flower store (triggering feelings of romance), she is more likely to give it to you than if you ask her outside a motorcycle store.

The environment is just as important as what you say.

Before the podcast began, I gave him a book as a gift: "The Anxiety of Influence," a history of poetry.

What would poetry have to do with influence and marketing?

In all art since the beginning of time, artists have built on the work of the artists who came before them.

Beethoven depended on a Mozart. Picasso depended on a Cézanne. Without Michelson, there would be no Einstein.

But poets, for some reason, would deny being influenced.

"I never even read Ezra Pound," shouted one poet at a critic. Poets want to be seen as original.

NOBODY is 100% original. This is the anxiety of influence.

Almost all of our decisions and even creativity are outsourced to the people around us who influence us: peers, teachers, religion, parents, bosses, etc.

Our personality is our own particular mishmash of influences.

How we deal with that anxiety, how we RECOGNIZE the influences, learn from them, build from them, is the birth of all of our creativity.

Let me summarize the seven aspects of influence:

1. *Reciprocity* – if you give someone a Christmas card, they will want to return the favor.
2. *Likability* – make yourself trustworthy. For instance, outline the negatives of dealing with you.
3. *Consistency* – ask someone for a favor. Now they will say to themselves, "I am the type of person who does James a favor."
4. *Social Proof* – if you are trying to get someone to do X, show them that "a lot of your peers do X." For instance, if you are at a bar and you are a guy trying to meet women, bring your women friends and not your guy friends with you.
5. *Authority* – "four out of five dentists say…"

6. *Scarcity* – "only 100 iPhones left at this store!"

7. *Unity* – you and I are the same because: location, values, religion, etc.

I've used each of the above in business. They work. They will make you money.

The entire purpose of language is to influence. We are not strong animals. We are weak. The language of influence saved us.

Probably a word like "run!" was the first word spoken. A word of influence. And it worked. I'm still running from the things I fear.

So speak to influence. Don't speak to call a flower yellow.

Speak to breathe spirit into an idea, to be enthusiastic, to convey emotion, to influence. This is the only way to have impact with your unique creativity.

I gave Robert the book as a gift ("reciprocity"), assuming we would have a great podcast. And we did.

But then I thought later, 'I can't even remember how Robert got on my podcast.' I highly recommended his book in the podcast and even in this chapter.

As he got into his car after the podcast in order to go to his next interview, I started thinking, 'Hmmm, who influenced whom?'

WHAT I LEARNED ABOUT NEGOTIATION FROM THE FBI'S BEST HOSTAGE NEGOTIATOR

They kidnap your husband and say they will kill him in 24 hours if you don't come up with a million dollars.

What do you do?

You call up Chris Voss, the former lead hostage negotiator for the FBI.

Chris has saved thousands of lives in hostage negotiations. He's negotiated against the world's most maniacal terrorists.

He worked for the FBI for 24 years.

Now he helps others negotiate. He helps companies, individuals, governments, etc.

He wrote an excellent book about negotiation called *Never Split the Difference*. I recommend it.

So I gave him a call. "Chris, how can I get better?"

He laughed when I met him. I said to him, "Did you fly here just to do this podcast?"

"I'm meeting the most interesting guy in the world," he said. "Why wouldn't I fly here?"

Flattery will get you nowhere! Nevertheless, I am effusively recommending his book,

And I got a chance to sit down with him and ask him everything

I wanted to know about negotiation.

I'm the worst at negotiating. I've lost companies, I've lost millions, I've lost time, I've gotten depressed—all due to bad negotiations.

I like to think that I learned from all the bad negotiations. Because at least in a bad negotiation, someone is good (the other side) and I can pick it apart and learn from it.

But much better was to simply meet the best negotiator in the world and ask him as many questions as I wanted.

"HOW?"

This is the most important thing I learned while talking to Chris.

You always want to get more information in a negotiation with as little commitment as possible on your side.

If one side says, "Show up with $1 million tomorrow," you can say, "How am I supposed to get you $1 million by tomorrow?"

They will keep talking.

Outsource the hard things they are asking right back to them.

If one side says, "We can only go as low as $36,000 on this car," you can say, "I can't go higher than $30,000. How am I supposed to come up with the $36,000?" And just see what they say.

Ask "open-ended questions" starting with "how" or "what." Ask a lot of them. Be prepared in advance with your "how" questions.

"NO"

A lot of people think you get people to say easy "yeses" so that when the situation gets more difficult, they are more primed to say "yes."

"Not true," Chris told me. "People are too primed now to say 'yes.' They know what you are up to. Get them to say 'no' first. That's the starting point."

How can I do that?

"Ask them a question like, 'Do you want this project to fail?' or 'Is this situation not going to work out for either side?'"

They don't want to fail, so they will say "no." Now you can start to find common ground.

LIST THE NEGATIVES

You can start to get empathy with the other side by listing the negatives on your side.

Then they start to agree with you.

For instance, you can say, "I know you might not trust me. I know you have had bad dealings in the past. I know you've had a hard childhood and this is the only way to make money."

They will say, "That's right." And once you have empathy with them, you can be a little more insistent on what it is you want.

POWERLESS

"Nobody wants to feel powerless. If the negotiation is not going your way you can say to them, 'Sounds like there's nothing you can do.'

"This will make them feel powerless. They will say 'no' to that and now they will try to do something for you to prove they are not powerless."

SPECIFIC NUMBERS

If someone says, "This car is $36,000," then come back with something like, "Listen, I know it's very difficult to go below $36,000. I know you are doing the best you can here. But the most I can afford is $32,157."

Then it appears (and it can also be true) that you are doing the homework and preparation to come up with an exact number that you can afford.

This is, of course, better if you have done the work to back up that specific number.

Then it is hard for them to fight it.

MIRROR

Whatever they say, repeat the last one to three words. Do this as much as possible.

If they say, "We can't go higher than $100,000 on salary because that's what everyone else is making," just say, "That's what everyone else is making," and see what they say next.

They will always say more.

Which goes along with:

SILENCE

Don't be afraid to go silent. Mirror and then have the confidence to go silent.

Nobody wants the negotiation to end. They will keep talking and give you more information.

Your goal is you want to get them talking as much as possible. The more information you have, the better. And the more likely they will negotiate against themselves.

DEADLINES DON'T MATTER

They need you as much as you need them. Most people don't realize that in the heat of a negotiation.

That's why they are in the negotiation in the first place.

If they put a deadline on, don't feel obligated to meet it. The negotiation won't end. They still need you.

THE POWER OF INFORMATION

"One time I was negotiating a hostage situation where they were asking for $1 million...

"Turns out the negotiations would intensify every Friday. How come? Because they really just wanted money to party all weekend.

"We ended up getting the negotiation down to $16,000 and by that time they had pretty much given up so the hostage was able to escape."

LATE-NIGHT FM DJ VOICE

This was a totally new one for me.

In Chris's book, "Never Split the Difference," he talks about how you have to use your "late-night FM DJ voice" when you negotiate to show people you are solid and serious.

I wasn't sure what that meant. He showed me. He got his voice about half an octave deeper and he slowed down a bit between each word.

I practiced. It worked. It was almost scary when I listened to Chris.

It brought back memories of my dad being super serious about punishing me and I did not want to mess with him.

TERMS AND CONDITIONS

This is where I have messed up the most in my own negotiations.

And, by the way, I am not innocent. I've sold, or been involved in the selling of, over a dozen companies.

I've negotiated many investments. Many sales of rights, inventions, patents, deals, etc.

I've been around the block. But I mess up. A lot. And "terms and conditions" are what get me.

For instance, it's not just a number for salary.

There can be more open-ended things that need to be discussed and put down on paper, like, "How can I best succeed at this job so I get a promotion/raise within a year?"

Or, "How can we work this out so I get an extra week vacation?"

In every situation there are extra terms and conditions that need to be worked out.

About 15 years ago, expert negotiator Dr. Larry Brilliant (his real name), who later became head of all of Google's charity work, gave me advice:

"Always make sure your list is bigger than theirs so you can give up the nickels in exchange for the dimes."

WHO THROWS OUT A NUMBER FIRST?

I have always gone back and forth on this. It's common sense to let them throw out a number first because maybe the number you throw out might be too low.

But then I used to figure that if I throw out a number first, it would be good for me because I can "anchor" them on a high number

"No," he said. "Let them throw out a number first."

For one thing, your number might be so high that they stop trusting you. And as far as anchoring, know what your range is and if their number is too low, don't let it anchor you.

"Be psychologically strong enough to not let them anchor you."
Also, if their number is too low, you can get back to the open-end-

ed "how" questions. Like, "If everyone else in my industry is paid 'X' then how can I go with the number you suggest?"

<hr />

PREPARATION

<hr />

Don't go crazy over this since you don't want to over-prepare. But get your "how"' questions ready. Your "no" questions.

List your negatives down on a piece of paper. Figure out your terms and conditions in advance.

Do some basic work so when you come up with specific numbers, you can back it up.

Make a preparation sheet.

I said to him, "You should be a couples' counselor." Thinking of the 10-plus couples therapists I've visited in the past 20 years.

Thinking of all the bad negotiations I've had in (now ex) relationships. Thinking of the hardships. The pain.

He laughed. "These techniques are good for all situations really. That's what I love about what I do."

I can't even imagine negotiating against him but he told me one story about working with his son.

One of his colleagues came to negotiate something with him. His son was there also.

They were talking for about an hour when his son started laughing. "Dad! Don't you see what he's doing? He's been mirroring everything you've been saying for the past hour and you just keep talking."

"I'm an assertive person," he said, "so it's easy to get me talking. My colleague was using my own tricks against me."

Even the master can be the student.

The key to success is to approach everything with humility. To know that there is always something new to learn in this surreal art of being human.

I think I'm too much of a sucker. I'm afraid every threat is true. And I want to please everyone. I want people to love me.

Next time my daughters negotiate with me I'm going to have to call Chris for coaching.

But maybe I will let them win anyway. Love will beat me in a negotiation every time.

THE TAO
of
LOUIS C.K.

Before I give a talk, I listen to Louis C.K. Before an interview. Before I write. Before I see my kids.

I first saw Louis C.K. perform in 1996. He was great. But sometime in the mid-2000s, he started to get more "honest." I don't know if that's the right word. I don't think he was ever dishonest.

But he had a routine that basically was "My kids suck," and he would list all the reasons why.

I played it for my kids. They were SHOCKED! My youngest said, "Did his kids hear this?" She was afraid for them.

(This was a while ago when my kids were still younger. They're much harder to shock now.)

I don't know if his kids heard it. It was true and it was funny and the reason my kids were shocked was because they were afraid that if I listened to this then their secret mission to drive me insane would be over.

Maybe it opened their eyes a tiny bit about how rotten little people can be. And guess what? Big people are pretty rotten also.

I listen to Louis C.K. not because he's funny (although it helps) but because he's right.

Life is hard, and things go wrong, and we constantly make mistakes and fool ourselves into thinking we have anything resembling common sense.

Louis C.K. is uncomfortable… and then he's not. Which is why we laugh.

Laughter has been around since before language. Mammals would use laughter to convey that a situation that they first thought was dangerous turned out not to be.

That rustle in the bushes? It was just a breeze. Not a lion.

He points it out. The contradictions in every day life. The contradictions I see in my life. The things that we're uncomfortable about.

Guess what? We don't have to be.

Here are some of his thoughts. And below are some of my interpretations.

....

1. *"What happens after you die?" "Lot's of things happen after you die—they just don't involve you."*

....

Ask at the end of the day, "Who did I help today?" instead of wondering about life after death.

That gives you a better life. Nothing will give you a better death.

....

2. *"'I'm bored' is a useless thing to say. You live in a great, big, vast world that you've seen none percent of."*

....

Take a walk. Read a book. Write down ideas. Ask someone you love what they are up to.

We now have non-stop entertainment. Unlike any other time in history. And my kids will still tell me they're bored.

Heck, I get bored.

But then I take a walk. And breathe. When I was a kid, I used to complain I was bored to my grandparents. I could've been more curious about them. Then they died.

I'm still alive.

---

3. *"When you have bacon in your mouth, it doesn't matter who's president."*

Mmmmm. Bacon. I miss it.

But the reality is: no opinion matters when you're eating bacon. No opinion matters when you're in the bathroom. Or kissing someone you love. Or when you're holding your breath for 20 seconds.

One time I was on a date and I actually told the date I was a big fan of Dan Quayle, only because she was a big fan.

Then when I tried to kiss her, she pushed me away. So what good was my opinion?

People worry about oil and fracking. Guess what? A solar-powered plane just flew across the country.

Whatever opinion you have, just sit back and smile and rest a little bit. The problem you are worried about will get solved. Or it won't. Chances are there's nothing you can do either way. So enjoy the bacon.

....

4. "People say, 'My phone sucks.' No, it doesn't! The shittiest cellphone in the world is a miracle. Your life sucks. Around the phone."

....

Blaming and complaining are draining. They never solve future problems and they only drain away energy from this moment.

We want that ugliness and fear that lives inside to be outside. We want to point the finger at it.

So we say, "He did it. He's an idiot! This phone sucks! My house is too small! My boss is a jerk!" and on and on.

Thoughts in our heads can't do anything. They are so invisible, not even a microscope can see them.

Only forward motion works. A superhero doesn't blame. A superhero flies through the sky and saves lives. Action!

....

5. "Self-love is a good thing but self-awareness is more important. You need to once in a while go, 'Uh, I'm kind of an asshole.'"

....

If you're great at ideas, or great at execution, but you eat poorly and are constantly sick, then you'll be constantly sick and never get anything done.

We're as good as our weakest link. Find the parts of your life where you can jump on the steepest learning curves and make that jump.

But many don't want to look at those weaknesses. I had always been bad at saying "no," but then I would blame other people for asking too much of me. Or I would feel overwhelmed and then I would get sick and anxious.
Instead, saying, "OK, I'm bad at telling people 'no," and then trying to improve it made me a lot happier and more relaxed.

By the way, I'm still bad at saying "no." The goal is not to wipe out all of your problems. You can't. There are no goals. There's just growth.

....

6. *"It doesn't have ANY effect on your life. What do you care?! People try to talk about it like it's a social issue. Like when you see someone stand up on a talk show and say, 'How am I supposed to explain to my children that two men are getting married?' I don't know. It's your shitty kid. You fuckin' tell 'em. Why is that anyone else's problem? Two guys are in love and they can't get married because you don't want to talk to your ugly child for five fuckin' minutes?"*

....

The key to the Tao of Louis C.K. is to not expend extra energy on things that don't matter, things that you can't change, things that you're being stupid about, things that won't be issues a billion years from now.

Instead, figure out the real issue: How do I talk to my kid, for instance? How do I talk to my wife? How do I avoid the people who are bringing me down? How do I stop wasting time thinking about these topics that are draining my energy?

Preserve energy for the people that need you. For the actions you can take that require all of that energy.

---

7. *"Everything that's difficult you should be able to laugh about."*

You always have two choices. Be anxious, or find joy in the situation in front of you.
Why waste any seconds of a preciously small life being anxious and afraid?

Everything has joy.

When I wake up in the morning, I try to practice this first thing: I think of the things the day before that made me happy. I feel how my body feels.

I let that feeling soak into all the cracks, all the places where I might be anxious or nervous or afraid. Mmmmmm.

Then I begin my day. Usually by watching a Louis CK show. Or, this morning, Amy Schumer.

8. *"Life's too short to be an asshole."*

The universe spent 14 billion years to get us to this perfect point, exactly as it was supposed to be.

Who am I to say, "You should be different," or "I'm better than you so I want THIS."

Because, in another flicker of time, we're just gone. And everyone left will be happy about it.

9. *"If a person is offended, then to them it is offensive. If someone else is not offended, then to them it isn't. They are both 100% right. For them."*

It's never my business what other people think.

If you ever want a lesson on this, look at any YouTube video and look at the comments.

Was it really worthwhile for those people to post hateful comments? Did they really change the world for the better by posting on a YouTube video among thousands of other comments?

Are they happy now?

10. *"I don't worry about how I'm doing, I just do what I'm doing."*

Doing my best in any situation is all I can do. If I worry about it while I'm doing it, I won't do my best.

The next day I will do my best also. If it doesn't work then OK, it's a perfect opportunity to learn.

As Mac Lethal said to me, "Nobody remembers your bad stuff, just keep working at it and you'll put out good stuff and that's what they will see and remember."

WHY DOES LOUIS C.K. KNOW SO MUCH?

I don't think he knows anything actually. And he doesn't pretend he does. The man who has nothing, has nothing to lose.

So that's why I listen. I want to be the man with nothing to lose.

PEOPLE DON'T REMEMBER WHAT THEY DON'T LIKE

S ometimes I get tense when I write something that I think people don't like.

Normally I don't care. But sometimes people actively hate things.

I called Mac Lethal. He's the fastest rapper in the world. He's gotten millions of views on his YouTube raps. Like his pancake rap. Or his Mozart rap. He did his ABCs rap on "Ellen."

I was fooled by the most basic myth of all: the overnight success. I thought that was the case with Mac Lethal but I was wrong.

We talked about how he'd been practicing for 17 years and developed his own breathing technique so he could make sounds during the inhale and exhale that were the words to his rap. The secret of his speed.

But then I asked him what I wanted to know for myself. How does he handle it when he does something he thought people would like but it turns out they don't?

He said it was very painful for him until he realized something.

"People don't remember what they don't like."

And then he went on to create the Mozart rap.

Which now has millions of views.

Thanks Mac!

HOW TO GIVE A GIFT

I t's hard to get good at life. I always try to get better but the universe of things I don't know versus the small things I do know is like 999,999,999,999 to 1.

I need many mentors. I need a new mentor every day.

I was talking to John Ruhlin. He did the best thing I ever heard of to get a mentor. Hal Elrod, author of "The Miracle Morning," started to tell me the story but I needed to find out directly.

So I picked up the phone, called John, and asked him to describe.

"I knew Cameron Herold was going to be in town and staying at the Ritz," he told me. "I also knew that he liked Brooks Brothers. And that he would probably be too tired to talk to me.

"So I called his assistant and got all his measurements. I went to Brooks Brothers and bought every shirt, every pair of pants, ties, etc. I tipped the manager at the Ritz $50 and before Cameron arrived we set up everything in Cameron's rooms.
Almost like a fashion show inside a hotel room. All the clothes on racks. He could pick whatever he wanted and I would return the rest. It cost me $7,000.

"After Cameron arrived he came down to meet me for our scheduled meeting. Instead of being tired, he was super excited. He couldn't believe what I had done for him. He picked out clothes and paid me back for everything. The guys at the Ritz returned the rest to Brooks Brothers.

"So it cost me nothing other than a few hours of time and now I have a mentor for life."

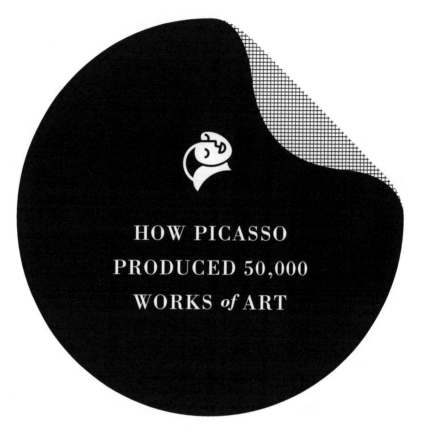

HOW PICASSO
PRODUCED 50,000
WORKS *of* ART

Barbara Cortland broke the world record. In 1983, she wrote 23 novels. She was 82 years old. Two novels a month that year.

Altogether she wrote 723 published novels. The last she wrote at age 97. When she died a year later, there were 160 unpublished novels still waiting to be published.

Did people like her work? Depending on what estimate you use, she sold between 600 million and 2 billion books. Most of her books were romance novels.

Was she creative? Was she an artist? I don't know if those questions matter.

She loved doing it, else she would not have done it. And people loved her work, else she would not have sold around a billion or so books. Is "art" a question or an answer?

Picasso might know. He said, "The less art there is in painting, the more painting there is."

In other words, just do it. Leave behind everyone else's definitions or else you will drown in them.

Why listen to him? He made 50,000 works of art in his life. On average two per day.

Is being prolific a requirement of being creative? No, not at all. Many great writers and artists have their master works and then they are done. Others, more prolific.

Jimi Hendrix made around 70 albums before he died at age 27.

Mozart composed over 600 pieces in his lifetime. Charles Schulz made 17,897 Charlie Brown strips before he died.

I want to be like them. The cruelest thing is that blank page each morning. To create something that never existed before completely out of nothing.

People say, "Everything has already been written." Everything has already been said.

But that's a lie.

I think every outline has already been written. But each human has a unique fingerprint.

Just putting that fingerprint on an outline makes it yours, different, unique. And through practice and vulnerability, you make that fingerprint something others want to see.

I don't know if there is such a thing as rules of creativity. I look back on the past 15 years. I've published 17 books and maybe 2,000-3,000 articles. And today I sit here and can't think of any "rules."

Fortunately I can steal some rules and splash my own pompous interpretation on them.

So I'll turn to Picasso and see what he has to say.

* * *

A. *"Unless your work gives you trouble, it is no good."*

I love this quote. "Trouble" means so many things. Maybe people will not like you. Maybe you are experimenting too much. Maybe the trouble is what you are doing too new.

How could Barbara Cortland write 700 romance novels? And they are all formulaic. But that is where the trouble begins.

In all 700 books, two lovers meet. But a problem happens that keeps them apart. Cortland had to come up with 700 different problems to keep her lovers apart. And then solve them.

In every thriller, John Grisham is required to have a scene where the hero is completely at the mercy of the villain. In every James Bond movie, Bond is tied up and about to die at the hands of the bad guy.

If they solve the problem in the same way each time, then they lose their creativity. The trouble is the artist has to solve the problem in a new way, different than any solution before it.

The bigger the trouble, usually the better the outcome.

I lost a lot of money when a business I was involved in failed. It was big trouble.

So I poured myself into other projects that I would've forgotten about or not cared about. The outcomes have been incredible. Thank you, bad company, for that horrendous loss.

Am I getting into enough trouble with this chapter?

The trouble with THIS chapter is that it is egotistical to write on creativity. Because what do I know? I know nothing.

So I solve it by passing the buck to Picasso and Barbara Cortland and Mozart and then I try to piece together the clues on creativity they left behind.

I am the student. They can be my teachers.

....

B. *"Learn the rules like a pro, so you can break them like an artist."*

....

Kurt Vonnegut did nothing correct in his novels. His peers before him would have elaborate plots, floral descriptions, deep characters.

In Vonnegut's classic, "Slaughterhouse Five," the hero is wimpy guy who goes in and out of time and space and in the middle of it all, experiences the slaughter of Dresden.

Despite the time travel and space travel, "Slaughterhouse Five" is ultimately a memoir that breaks all the rules.

But Vonnegut said, "You can't break the rules of grammar until you know the rules of grammar."

He only wrote the book after many years of following the traditional "rules" of science fiction and more traditional fiction writing.

As Shawn Coyne wrote in "The Story Grid," every genre has its obligatory scenes. Don't break them. Be creative around them.

When Luke was at the mercy of Darth Vader...BAM!

"I am your father."

But is that art then? If we follow a formula? Shawn makes the point that Steve Jobs followed the very strict genre of the phone before making an iPhone, a work of art.

Elon Musk followed the whole genre of the car before making his first Tesla.

There's magic in taking what's been done a billion times before and doing it your way.

....

C. *"Action is the foundational key to all success."*

....

I know too many people who have an idea for a book, or a show, or a business. But they always say something like, "I'll do it when I have time" or "it's too late for me" (ignoring that Barbara Cortland wrote 23 books in her 82nd year).

The one thing in common from anyone above is that they practiced their art every single day. It's hard to sit down every day and... sit. Blank paper. Blank canvas. Blankness.

And then... if you do something... it might suck. It might be the worst thing you ever do.

Kobe Bryant, one of the greatest basketball players of all time, has an incredible world record: he's missed over 13,000 shots—more than any other player in professional basketball.

So taking action is more important than anything else.

Nothing > Thinking > Doing > Finishing > Repeating as a daily practice for... I don't know.

But I hope I can do it every day.

....

D. *"To copy others is necessary, but to copy oneself is pathetic."*

....

I wrestle with this. People ask me what's a common problem for me. This is a problem.

Sometimes I look back at a post and think, "People liked that. I should do that style again."

I hate that feeling.

I need to do "D" more often. Every time Picasso felt comfortable, he changed styles completely. His blue period is nothing like cubism is nothing like his surrealism (see "Drawing for Guernica").

I'm sure each period borrows from the others. But he was not a lone genius.

While Picasso may be the father of cubism, he was standing on the shoulders of Cézanne and Matisse, both learning from them and competing with them, trying to outdo what they had done before.

He copied them, and left his old style behind, forming a new meld, which became what we now think of as cubism. And then he left that behind, never to return to it.

To be fair, Barbara Cartland, perhaps did copy herself too much. The last two decades of her life, while prolific, resulted in fewer sales. But who can say? She loved what she did and wanted to keep doing it.

On the same topic, Picasso once said, "Success is dangerous. One begins to copy oneself, and to copy oneself is more dangerous than to copy others. It leads to sterility."

I need to figure out what to do next. Maybe that's why I'm exploring all of these masters of reinvention.

Reinvention is scary. And it's risky. But it is unavoidable. I'm scared right now.

E. *"The chief enemy of creativity is good taste."*

When "50 Shades of Grey" was on its way to selling 40 million copies, everyone hated it.

I wrote an article about why it was a great work of literature. I got emails that said, "This is why America is falling apart. People with no education are liking drivel like this."

OK.

And yet 40 million people thought reading it would make their lives better. Meanwhile National Book Award finalists will maybe sell about 5,000 copies.

Sales aren't everything. I get it. And sometimes a work of art can be intended for the few and not the many.

But the arbiters of taste are all using the past as their metrics. The future is still a blank slate. Else we'd be there.

F. *"Everything you can imagine is real."*

Elon Musk wants to die on Mars. "Just not on impact," he says.

OK, maybe he will and maybe he won't. But he made a rocket that can get him there. The first advance in rocket technology in 40 years.

He's making batteries and solar cells that can fuel the rocket. He's launched rockets into space and built electric cars that can go from 0 to 60 in 3.2 seconds.

I don't know. Maybe he will get there.

One time I wanted to pitch an idea directly to the CEO of HBO. On the way there, I ran into a friend of mine and told her where I was going.

She said, "You can't do that!" I couldn't just go over my boss and his boss and his boss and his boss and his boss.

But I did.

And he said "yes."

Most of the time, people say "no." In almost everything I've done, I've gotten 20 "no"s for every "yes."

Is this good or bad? Maybe I should try to get more "yesses. OK. I'll try. Maybe it will happen.

Picasso also says, "I am always doing things I can't do—that's how I get to do them."

My daughter lost a tennis match the other day at school.

I asked her, "What did you learn?"

She said, "What do you mean? I was disappointed."

If she always sticks to only what she can do (a safe, consistent serve instead of a harder one that will miss more) then she will never get better at what, right now, she can't do.

It's the "can'ts" that add up to a win or a loss. The "cans" just keep you in the box of what's safe.

In 1953, Picasso gave up painting—he thought forever. For the first time in his life, he started writing poetry. Then singing.

Was he good? Probably not. He went back to painting. But he turned a "can't" into an "I did it."

"Accidents, try to change them—it's impossible. The accidental reveals man."

Real life is not in a self-help book. Or in an article on the 10 ways to be a leader.

It's the accidents that allow you to measure who you are as a person. Or as a creator. It's when betrayal and disappointment visit you that you can test what you are made of, process it, transform it.

I wonder sometimes if people can change. Because normally I don't like people who do things that I find dishonest.

But I've been dishonest. I've been despicable. I hope I can change.

HOW TO PUT THESE QUOTES TO WORK?
HOW TO BE CREATIVE?

For me: I have my daily routine.

I wake up and I'm grateful. I try to think every day of new things to be grateful for.

I sleep well, exercise, and try to eat well.

I try to love the people in my life. It's hard. There are "accidents." But maybe it gets easier with practice.

I try to be creative.

I bow down and surrender to what I can't control.

And then at each of these things, I try to improve 1%—which means nothing; what is the math of gratitude?

But here's the math. Compounding 1% a day in X, makes X 38 times better in a year.

Because this 1% gets me in that scary void of "can't." How can I be most grateful when a business fails? Or someone sends me hate mail?

How?

And then I sit here. And I try to find a new vein to bleed from. Or I take everything in my house and throw it away. Sometimes that works also.

HOW TO FIND YOUR
CALLING

He died. He was giving a speech, sat down, and the next thing... he was dead.

They called an ambulance. The paramedics did that thing. They brought him back to life.

But his body didn't like living.

He died again. Eight more times they used machines to convince the machine in his body that we call a heart to come back to life.

"Please come back to life," the machines said to his heart. And finally his heart decided to stay.

After that, things changed. Like they often do when we die at the age of 47.

"There are three things," Chip Conley, now the head of hospitality for Airbnb, told me. "A job, a career, and a calling.

"I had been building and running hotels for 20 years. It was my calling to be in the hospitality business. I built over 50 hotels. But it was starting to feel like a job.

"When I died, I realized I couldn't do it anymore. I had to go back to my calling."

Within a few years he had sold his business. He had nothing left to do.

"I had faith in my calling, though," Chip said. "Something would happen."

And it did. It did.

*   ✦   ✦

ADAM WROTE ME.

He was my Airbnb host. I've been in four different Airbnbs that Adam owns over the past three years.

So we knew each other. I only live in Airbnbs and I know many of the regular hosts in New York City.

"I'm having a special guest in the apartment right downstairs from you," Adam wrote me. "He's the head of all hospitality for Airbnb. Would you like to meet?"

Yes, very much so. I had spent 90% of my life in Airbnbs over the prior three years and just about 100% in the last year. In 2014 I even wrote an article, "10 Ways to Improve Airbnb."

Adam made the introduction. Chip Conley, the man who had died a few years earlier and sold his hotel business, responded.

"Should I bring a bottle of wine?" he asked. He came upstairs and we started to talk.

"Brian Chesky, the founder of Airbnb, called me and asked me if I wanted to be the head of hospitality. Airbnb was a tech company, it wasn't used to being a hospitality company.

"When I ran 50 hotels, hospitality was my main focus. For each hotel, I had the hotel managers come up with five adjectives for what that hotel would be. Maybe the adjectives might be: funky, hip, modern, clean, rock 'n' roll.

"Every employee, even the housekeepers, would keep those adjectives in mind in whatever they did. And, if possible, we even made sure the five senses the customers would experience in the hotels would match the five adjectives."

"This is a great idea," I said. "You can even apply ideas like this to writing a book. Or even building a career for yourself. What five adjectives do you want to describe your life, or the objects you create, or your relationships?"

"Absolutely," Chip said.

So he went to Airbnb to start creating an atmosphere of hospitality among the hosts.

He had found his way back to his life's calling.

I've felt it since 2013. Now I live in them. Now they are home.

All because Chip died.

*　＊　*

"HOW DO YOU FIND YOUR LIFE'S CALLING?" I ASKED CHIP.

"What did you love doing when you were 6, 8, 10 years old?" he said. "Like I had one friend who even at 6 was making mud pies as if they were real pies. Then she became a lawyer but was always unhappy. So she quit being a lawyer and is now one of the biggest pastry chefs in the world.

"For me, I was always pretending to run a restaurant in my house. I always wanted to be in the hospitality business."

I thought back to when I was 10 years old. I was writing short stories. And when I was 12, I even wrote an article in the newspaper interviewing politicians.

You find your interests from back then and see how they age into the current day.

"Find the thing you did where you lost all sense of time while you are doing it," Chip told me.

"Remember the equation from Victor Frankl's *Man's Search for Meaning*.

"Despair = Suffering - Meaning.

Find the things that bring you meaning. Suffering is always there in this world. But if you have meaning, you will have less despair. You will find your calling."

Sometimes even now I find myself doing things where I feel more "job" than "calling." I try to adjust where I can, but it can be difficult. I guess a little bit at a time and eventually you can move your life into that calling.

I said to him, "This is too good. Do you mind if I record the conversation?"

He said, "Sure."

So I did.

I've been recording conversations with people ever since I was 10 years old.

* * *

"WHEN I WAS 26," HE SAID.

"I wanted to be an entrepreneur. I founded my first little motel and called it the Phoenix.

"I knew that whatever I did, I wanted to be creative and to have freedom. I tell everyone to write down the two most important qualities about their calling and check back with it over the years.

"Eventually I felt like what I was doing was the opposite of creativity and freedom. And that's when I had that experience of flat-lining. That was my body's way of telling me I had to change. So I got rid of my hotels."

"What if you are sitting in a cubicle and listening to this and wondering how you can find that creativity and freedom for yourself?" I asked. "It all sounds good BUT kids, responsibilities, age, etc. you feel are blocking you?"

"Then get back to what you loved when you were younger. Start to brainstorm how you can bring that even a little bit into your life now. And a little bit more the next day. And so on.

"Try many things. One thing I realized is that quantity equals quality. People think it's one or the other but it's not. When you have a quantity of ideas and things you are trying, you will find quality."

This reminded me of my approach to exercising my idea muscle. If you write down 10 ideas a day, you have 3,650 ideas in a year. And maybe one or two will be good.

After he left, I thought about what I most wanted to do when I was a kid.

I wanted to be a spy.

On whom? I don't know. I just wanted to look at other people and follow them without them knowing. To observe and learn all of their secrets and then report back to "H.Q.»

It would be a little dangerous, I always thought. But I would survive. And save the world.

Bit by bit I'm doing it. My calling.

+ − ○

ARE YOU A PLUS, A MINUS, OR A ZERO?: LESSONS FROM AN ASTRONAUT

[CHRIS HAS A DIFFERENT BUT EQUALLY VALID, DEFINI-TION OF PLUS MINUS ZERO]

" There are three types of people," astronaut Chris Hadfield told me. "-1, 0, and +1."

Chris Hadfield spent 166 days in space in the space station ISS.

While there he also sang "Space Oddity" and uploaded the video to YouTube, where it was viewed 33 million times.

When a business fails it feels like a -1. When a relationship fails, often it's because I've been a -1. Certainly stalking and begging and crying have made me a -1 many times.

When I clam up in my shell, afraid to return calls, afraid to admit responsibility, that's -1 behavior. When I think I'm a +1, often I'm a -1.

Even worse, much worse, is when other people think you are a -1.

There's a saying: "It's none of my business what people think of me."

But sayings are fun to say and hard to live.

When people think I'm a -1, I have a tendency to add all of those people up. My insecurity wants them to like me.

Sometimes that makes me a -1,000.

Being a +1 is usually difficult to me. I never know what I'm doing.

For instance, one time I was CEO of a company that was my idea. I was very good at raising money. We raised $30 million.

I had no idea how much money we made. What our costs were. I didn't even know what our product did. I had bought it with the money we raised.

I was so afraid to talk to people, I would get in early and lock the door behind me and not answer the door when people knocked.

Eventually they fired me as CEO. Then they fired me from the board. Then they took my shares away. I went from a +1 to a -1 very quickly.

It's good to be a zero sometimes. To learn and listen and help.

When I do a podcast, I feel like a zero.

I ask people to come on my podcast because I want to learn something from them. How to be a better person. They are +1 people. I'd like to be like them. So I ask them questions.

Here are the qualities of a zero.

* **LISTEN** to what people tell you. Maybe they experienced something you have never experienced. Our brain can curate the experiences of others so maybe it can help us live our own lives better.
* **OBSERVE** what people do. We have what are called "mirror neurons." If I think I'm a +1 at firing a gun, I might shoot myself and kill myself.

If I watch someone over and over firing a gun, then my mirror neurons kick in and I might be able to do it myself if asked.

Although I hope nobody asks me.

* **BE HUMBLE.** Some people are great people. They are kind. They are humble. They are productive. They are competent. They get things done. Then they get AMAZING things done.

When you compare, you despair. When you are humble, you learn. When you get curious, you get better.

How did they get this way? Oh! They read some books. They wrote some books. They had some ideas. They worked hard every day for years. They saved some lives.

OK, now I've learned from them. Maybe I can do some of that also. One-tenth of that if I'm lucky.

* **BE CURIOUS.** A zero starts with:
* What are they doing?
* How are they doing it?
* How can I help?
* How can I get better?
* How can I be competent? Then build trust? Then build excellence?

* **HAVE THEMES INSTEAD OF GOALS.** Chris Hadfield wanted to be an astronaut for 21 years before he became the

commander of the International Space Station for 166 days. Sometimes he had disappointments along the way.

"If I had only focused on big successes," he said, "then I would be disappointed most of the time. You have to focus on the small successes and make sure to celebrate them."

He had a theme of being competent. Of helping the astronaut program. Of being an astronaut. Of working toward the common goals of a program he believed in. He achieved many small successes that way.

And then he sang "Space Oddity" while circling Earth 2,600 times in a row on a 92-million-mile trip he took. Watch it on YouTube. It's great.

People tend to think they are meant for something BIG in their lives. I understand that. But to get to BIG you have to focus on today.

I have to keep quoting Chris. "Continually investing in the success of others is what will eventually lead to success for yourself."

* **BE RESPECTFUL.** One person can lead a company. But it takes thousands of employees, customers, investors, fans, etc. to really create a success.

A good follower observes the leader, trusts his suggestions, and then ties his own success to the success of the company.

When I worked at HBO, I only started to feel like I was

accomplishing something when my language changed from "they" (referring to HBO) to "we."

I was a zero there. But I watched all of the shows, learned enough of the vision, learned the company's history, followed the lead of its executives, until I could make my own contribution.

My contribution was big enough that other companies started to approach me and ask me if I could help them also.

So I started my first company. I haven't had a job since.

* **DON'T BE ENTITLED.** I admit, sometimes I get angry feeling like a zero. I want to be a +1 all the time, at everything I do.

I get competitive. I want to be the best at this, or the best at that. RIGHT NOW.

One thing I know for sure is that feeling entitled to anything will automatically put a ceiling on what you get out of life.

Do you know someone who is feeling entitled? Is he angry most of the time? Entitled people are the ones who later say, "I should've been X" and they are bitter and then life is over.

Entitlement. Ceiling. Entitlement. Ceiling. I have to remind myself of that all the time. A +1 with entitlement can become a -1 within seconds.

It's important to realize that what's most important is paying attention to the things that are not important.

* **DON'T BE DISAPPOINTED.** One time Chris Hadfield had a serious setback when France gave away his slot for its test pilot program to another person for political reasons.

He was disappointed. He thought he wouldn't be an astronaut. Then he heard Air Canada was hiring pilots. He considered taking a job there.

His wife, Helene, said, "You don't really want to be a pilot. You wouldn't be happy and then I wouldn't be happy. Don't give up on being an astronaut. I can't let you do that to yourself or to us."

So he didn't go for the job and he ended up in outer space.

Sometimes $0 + 0 = +1$.

This isn't a story about math. Or being a success. Or being an astronaut. Or achieving all your dreams.

This is a love story.

WHAT I LEARNED ABOUT PHOTOGRAPHY FROM CHASE JARVIS

I suck at photography.

I take a photo and it looks like puke. It looks dead. I wish I were better.

Chase Jarvis is a great photographer. He's won all sorts of awards. I wanted to talk to him.

So I lied. He asked me if he could interview me for "Chase Jarvis Live," his web show where he's interviewed hundreds of people. I said "yes" but I had only one motive.

I don't like being interviewed. It feels embarrassing. I don't think I have anything to teach anyone. I've fallen so many times that I'm now broken.

I'm OK with that. That's not what this is about.

I went to the interview. There were lights, camera, action. Chase asked, "Who are you?" to get me talking.

So I changed direction, "But first, I have to ask you, what can you tell me so that within one hour I can leave here and take the best photo I've ever taken?"

He laughed. I didn't want to answer any questions. I wanted to ask.

If I can't listen, I can't learn. If I am speaking, I can't listen. If I am answering, I'm not asking.

"First, find out what your filter is. Do you like taking pictures of people, buildings, nature?"

Easy.

"Sad people," I said.

"OK. Go out on the street. Find someone you feel some sort of connection with before you take their picture. But try to be as close to them as possible."

"How do I get close up though? Won't that be weird?"

"Here's what you do. Just go and talk to them. Say, 'I've been having a hard time lately with grief. When I saw you I felt an instant connection and felt like you could understand and I would really like to take your picture.' "

I never thought about talking to them. I always thought of photographs as somehow being taken secretly.

"Won't that make them pose?"

"No, you're building a connection. It's almost like you're sharing a story. They will relate to you. You have to get good at connecting with people in 10 seconds."

More important than technique. More important than equipment. More important than the angle or the sunlight or the details of the photo was simply the art of connection.

Two people connecting can create a work of art. Nothing else. I liked that.

People sometimes ask me, "What software do you use to write?"

I use Facebook status updates. And I make sure I have something to say.

After we were finished, I went outside and saw a woman that looked interesting.

I asked her where she was from. She said Mexico. I asked her since she was from Mexico, what were her feelings about Donald Trump?

She said, "I'm for Donald Trump."

I said, "You might be the only Mexican ever who is for Donald Trump."

She said, "Everyone is the same. I'm sick of the same. Maybe he will do something different. Change is important."

Not all change is the same, but I left it at that.

I said, "Show me your tattoo."

She had a tattoo of an elephant on her arm. She picked up her sleeve so I could see all of it. She told me sometimes she and her husband have had hard times.

I said, "Can I take your photo?"

She said yes.

So I took her photo.

It wasn't a good photo. But it was my first attempt at taking a photo based on connection.

Today I will try again. And tomorrow. And then the next day. If I don't get better, I will at least have fun trying. And what else is there in life but to play as much as possible?

Every attempt at art depends first on connection. Every business depends on connection.

When I tried the original iPod, I listened to all of the music I loved as a kid. I was walking around with a smile all day.

Steve Jobs somehow connected with me through that iPod.

I've read my favorite book of stories over 300 times. I fall in love with it each time. It's about characters that seem so lost, but they hang onto their lives through their connection with each other. I can relate to that.

If I want to sell an idea, if I want to convince, if I want someone to like to me, I have to figure out how to connect.

The only skill for survival and success is having that ability to connect.

I'm glad I learned something from Chase. My ego hopes he learned something from me but I don't know.

"Everyone always asks me what camera I use," Chase said. "But greatness is about storytelling."

7

SEVEN THINGS I LEARNED FROM MY EIGHT GREATEST TEACHERS

I thought about going to my 25th high school reunion. I wanted to go. I had a car key and I could've driven there. I was close to feeling like I was going to do it. But I was feeling somewhat shy. I didn't like high school much.

When you are rejected so much, you build a tough skin.

My eight greatest teachers in life were perhaps the many girls in high school who said "no" to me when I was desperate to go out with them. Who knows what would've happened to me if everything were easy then. Maybe I would not have been able to handle it when things became really hard later.

I liked a girl in my drawing class. Nadine Davis. But when I asked her out she quickly said "no" and walked away. It was like one of those scenes in a movie, where she disappeared into the crowd and everyone around me was sort of whispering and smirking. If she had asked, I probably would've paid her to go out with me.

I liked a girl who had thick curly orange hair. I forget her name now. Michelle? I played one of those games. I told her I knew someone who liked her. So for a week we kept up that intrigue and she was always smiling at me and wanting to know who. And then when I told her it was me, she turned the other way and wouldn't look back at me.

Finally one of the football players walked over to her and said, "Do you need help?"

She said, "I'm OK." I walked away then.

There was another girl I liked who was sort of ditzy but she was smarter than she let on. I told a friend of mine who was friends with her that I liked her. The message was conveyed to the girl I liked and I got a message back.

"Maybe in 100 years I would consider it."

Somehow I was encouraged by that. It wasn't a solid "no!" It's been almost 30 years now. Just 70 more years to go. The only problem is I can't remember her name, so I'm not sure how I'd find her.

There was a girl I liked who was a year older than me. We had a fun time talking and had a good mutual friend. The mutual friend told me, "You have a chance here."

But then the girl I liked started going out with someone else and I think they're even married now. Or dead. Who knows?

There was a girl I had a massive lust-crush on who lived around the corner from me and she was even in my Hebrew school carpool when we were younger. Her mom was always screaming at her as she rushed out the door in the morning, usually five minutes late so the bus would sit there and wait while she and her mom finished their yelling.

My friend Robert also liked her and they used to ride bikes together. But maybe she was a "beard" because it turned out later that Robert was gay. Maybe he's dead now. I can't find him on Facebook or anywhere and we were best friends for 12 years.

I finally got a girl to go out with me. I was in 12th grade and she was in 11th grade. I had not only been accepted to college but I had just won New Jersey's junior chess championship. So even though no chess player should ever have the right to feel confident with girls, this time I felt confident and she said yes.

The day we were supposed to go out it was snowing, so my dad wouldn't let me drive the car. I was supposed to pick her up at school.

There were no cell phones then so all I could do is picture her standing out there in the deepening snow waiting for me while I sat home begging and crying with my dad despite the fact that I was the 18-year-old New Jersey junior chess champ. Relegated to crying like a little baby so I could drive a car.

A month later, without any snow on the ground, I got in my first car accident.

I liked the girl with the paper route next to mine in 10th grade. I, of course, asked her out and she said "yes."

And I was like, "Really?" and I was very happy.

But the next day, her brother came over to me to tell me she was just saying that so as not to disappoint me.

I walked straight out of the school and over to Steve Giacalona's house where he was recovering with a broken leg. He had been run over by a friend of ours who had gone crazy and we never saw again.

He was having regular sex at that point, even with his broken leg. I asked him if he thought any girl would ever like me. He told me the truth and said probably not but I should smile a lot.

There was the girl in English class. Debbie. I did the usual trick: became friends with her friend and had the message transmitted. They lost their friendship as a result. That's how bad it was to say, "I like James." My first kiss had to wait until I was in college.

WHAT I LEARNED:

* I learned how to handle "no."
* I learned how to ask.
* I learned that I had to be stand out in some way.
* I learned to be polite to other people who found themselves rejected in various ways.
* I learned how to better sell myself (a variation on "standing out").
* I learned to be persistent. That love (or anything) is a quantity game before whittling down to quality.
* I also learned that time heals everything. Almost all of the above are Facebook friends now. So, at the end of the day, every emotion gets watered down with age. And even a "no" forms an attachment through time.

*   *   *

I don't have many friends that I see on a daily or even yearly basis. It's so easy to lose track. But it's also so easy to keep track now that we have social media.

Which is why I like Facebook. I've made friends through Facebook and can see what's going on with people I used to know.

Now with just a few clicks I can sit here in the dark at 3 a.m. and see that Joanne Arico from elementary school has made a new friend.

Good for her. It's nice to have new friends.

13

THIRTEEN THINGS WAYNE DYER PERSONALLY TAUGHT ME

I was scared to death. Wayne Dyer was going to come on my podcast. I read about 10 of his books. I watched five or six of his PBS specials.

The man has sold over 150 million books. He's inspired millions. He's already given hundreds of interviews. What could I possibly ask him?

I watched other interviews with him. I even spoke to his daughter about him.

I wanted to be ready. I didn't want to ask the same questions everyone else was asking.

"You have to interrupt him," a friend told me, "or he will keep on talking."

So probably the first thing is: I learned how to interrupt people.

Afterward, the guy who did the audio for the podcast said to me, "That was unbelievably inspiring." And then he quit his job.

Wayne Dyer has worn many hats. He's been a therapist, a professor, a writer, a PBS fundraiser, and, to many, a spiritual leader.

I have no idea what he is. I think he wore many hats because in an interesting life, you do many interesting things.

The dots don't always have to connect.

To me he is the ultimate "Choose Yourselfer."

He started out dirt poor as an orphan coming out of foster homes. He went to school, got his PhD, became a professor, and was so loved by his students he reached tenure by age 35, in 1975.

Do you know what tenure is? It means the school has to pay you for the rest of your life. It means you never have to worry about a job or money again. You're set.

So what did he do then?

He quit.

He had written a book, *Your Erroneous Zones*, and it failed in his eyes. It had sold 5,000 copies. When a book sells 5,000 copies the publisher typically wipes their hands clean (they have made a tidy profit) and says, "OK, on to the next one."

That wasn't good enough. He didn't want a publisher to choose whether he was a success or not.

He quit his 100% safe job. Most people's jobs are not safe. He had one of the few that actually are. Everyone said he was crazy and begged him not to.

He bought out the rest of the inventory of books from his publisher and put them in the trunk of his station wagon.

With his 9-year-old daughter sitting next to him, he drove all over the country, from bookstore to bookstore, begging them to take his books.

You choose yourself one choice at a time. You choose yourself every day. You choose yourself with all of your fears and hopes mixed together and nobody knows what's going to happen.

But if you do it with a sense of mission, a belief in your vision, what happens may not be what you expect, but you will never say, "I wonder what would have happened..."

He has sold over 100 million books since then.

Before I did the podcast, I spoke about Wayne Dyer to a friend of mine who I thought would be very skeptical. My friend is the CEO of a company that does $200 million in revenues a year.

"Wayne Dyer is like a hero to me," he said. I was curious why.

"Think of it this way: he's done 10 specials raising money for PBS. He's raised over $150 million for PBS."

"That is impressive," I said.

"Yes, but that's not the point. PBS runs those pledge shows over and over. And PBS has higher ratings than all of the broadcast channels combined. Think about how much airtime and free advertising Wayne Dyer got for himself by doing those shows."

I don't think that's why Dyer did those shows but it's an interesting perspective.

There's nothing wrong with raising money, inspiring millions, and also helping yourself. That's what the CEO was pointing out to me.

Here are 13 things Wayne Dyer told me that I learn from every day:

A) DO WORK YOU BELIEVE IN SO MUCH YOU'D GO TO JAIL FOR IT

When "Your Erroneous Zones" came out, it was banned in all of the countries behind the Iron Curtain. So Dr. Dyer smuggled copies into Prague. That's how much he believed in the message he was spreading.

B) LOOK AT YOUR LIFE FROM A DISTANCE

Dr. Dyer grew up in an orphanage, an incredibly hard experience and one that many people might not be able to overcome.

But difficult experiences are what sculpt the soul. Now he's thankful, he told me, for those experiences.

C) GO TO THE PEOPLE

At the beginning of his career, someone told Dr. Dyer, "The only way to reach everyone in America is by getting on a nationally syndicated TV show."

No matter how many times he contacted the big shows, they rejected him every time.

So he packed his car full of books and drove across the whole country to connect with people face to face.

Today everyone wants to "go viral." They want the Internet to make them an overnight success. But sometimes you just need to work insanely hard and go to the people. One at a time, face to face.

"Viral" often is a disease you want to get rid of. But "connection" can lead to lifelong benefits.

D) "ARRANGE WHATEVER PIECES COME YOUR WAY"

He said everyone today is so eager to blame their situation on the stock market or the economy.

But whatever meager resources you have, make it work for you. Find a way to move forward.

He said that since he was 9 years old, he's never been unemployed, even if it meant he had to carry bags of groceries at the supermarket for a nickel.

The key to an enriched life is to have a burning desire. Wayne says that you must "have an inner flame that, no matter what goes before you, it never flickers."

This desire will enable you to seize every opportunity and create the life you want to live.

Don't let someone tell you can't do XYZ because there's no money in it.

"People used to tell me, 'Don't be a teacher, you can't make any money doing it,'" he told me.

But now he says he's a teacher with the largest classroom and the most amount of students.

Every day, don't try to jump into another box. Just try to think a little bit more outside of the box society has put you in.

E) ALWAYS TAKE RESPONSIBILITY FOR YOUR OWN LIFE

Wayne says that if something isn't working in his life, he always tells himself, "It must be because I haven't used enough determination or I haven't been fearless enough or I haven't been willing to do whatever it takes to make it happen."

He never lets himself make any excuses. Because even if there is an external explanation, he can't control external factors. He can only control himself.

F) "LEAVE YOURSELF OPEN TO WHATEVER COMES UP"

On June 26, 2013, Wayne announced to his whole family that he was done writing books.

He explained in great detail why he felt like that chapter of his life was done.

Then on June 27, he started writing his next book. He had 100% intended to be done with books, but when he felt the urge to start writing that morning, he embraced it.

Rather than resisting and forcing his own plans, he accepted what came his way and let it direct him.

G) WE ARE "DOOMED" TO MAKE OUR CHOICES

There are some things that we can't change. Our hardwiring, our bodies, our physical limitations.

But within that framework we have the power to make choices. We choose how to use the resources we were given.

Improving (or not improving) 1% a day is not even noticeable. That's why it's so easy for people to say, "Nothing is happening," and inadvertently cost their lives 1% a day. Focus on that 1% improvement and everything changes.

H) HOW TO FIND YOUR LIFE PURPOSE

You might be saying, "OK, James, a bunch of these lessons are about following your purpose, but what if I don't know what mine is?!"

Wayne asked, "What's the difference between good and God?"

The answer is "O." Not just 'oh' but 'zero.'

So whatever makes you feel good, whatever energizes you and lights you up inside, that's God. That's God telling you that that's what you are meant to be doing.

I don't believe that anyone has one purpose in life. And I don't like attaching any one religious philosophy to being content in life.

But I like the idea of taking that "zero" and filling it up, if only for today, with something you love.

I) "SELL YOUR CLEVERNESS AND CREATE A SENSE OF AWE"

Life is a gift. Don't let your ego get in the way of fully experiencing and appreciating it.

When we were kids, we laughed and asked question. As adults, we cry and shout answers.

Sometimes it's good to feel like a kid again, even at age 75.

J) DON'T REGRET YOUR LIFE

Wayne said to me, "The number one regret of the dying is 'I wish I had the courage to live the life I wanted rather than doing what others wanted of me.'"

It's hard living the life you want. It requires determination and strength and wisdom and fearlessness. And those are all difficult things.

You only find the alternative waiting for you on your deathbed.

K) ENLIGHTENMENT

Not in a woo-woo, intangible way with no connection to the real world. Too many people try to scam with that word.

"Enlightenment is all about improving your relationships. Being more loving with your spouse. Being more patient with your children. The quest for enlightenment is about improving your daily life in real ways."

L) "THERE ARE THREE WAYS TO ENLIGHTENMENT"

Suffering: reflecting on pain in the past and learning from it; Being present: learning from what you're going through right now; "Getting out front": being proactive rather than reactive.

M) "THERE IS A SECRET GARDEN WITHIN US"

No matter what happens in the world around us, no matter what happens to us, there is a place inside of you where you are 100% in control of what happens.

"Maybe you can't control the terrible things that happen to you, but you're in control of how you respond."

You're in control of your feelings and your own happiness. That's not to say that it's not incredibly difficult, but the point is that NO ONE ELSE has the power over your mindset. "Inside your chest, you are sovereign."

*   *   *

I WAS SORT OF IN A GLOW AFTER THE INTERVIEW.

I was excited. I felt like doing a podcast was the right thing. I wasn't sure until then.

Maybe most the important thing I learned was one thing he said to me toward the end: "Are you willing to do whatever it takes to make the thing that excites you come true? Are you fearless?"

I'll be honest: I don't know. Sometimes it's very hard. Sometimes crisis hits and you can't move.

I think that's OK. Sometimes you have to take a rest to re-energize.

But I have faith that his final words to me are the trick: "Come from a place of compassion and love."

5

FIVE THINGS I LEARNED
FROM SUPERMAN

I jumped off the bed, flew into the air, and landed the wrong way on my foot, breaking it. I was 6 and there was every indication I was from the planet Krypton, whose sun exploded when I was a baby, leaving me an orphan on a planet filled with people who would never fully understand me

I had a cape on (my Superman blanket). The weak gravity of Earth would not hold me down. Nothing could hold me down.

My mother claims she heard the crack of bone from the other side of our suburban house. Crack! I landed. It could've happened. She might've heard it.

I had to wear a cast. On the first day of first grade, in a brand new school, I was "that kid." The one who limped. The one who had a cast. You know, the one you probably would've hung out with because clearly I was destined to be the coolest kid in first grade.

At the end of the day I had an itch inside my cast. It was excruciating. And it was raining. The teacher, Mrs. Klecor, wouldn't let us leave to catch our bus at the end of the day unless we could spell our names.

I have a bad name for such a task. "Altucher."

I was sure I was going to miss my bus. I was the last one left. I started to cry. Because after school I was getting the cast off. But not if I couldn't spell my name and I missed my bus.

Almost 30 years later, I'm still Superman.

I'm clumsy like Clark Kent. I have glasses. Black hair. I'm often shy in public. People often laugh at me.

And, like many people, I have a secret identity that I'm hiding. One that I reveal bit by bit. But if I were to reveal everything I'd end up in jail or a hospital or an institution or more people would hate me than already do or other people would be badly hurt by those who would take advantage of the real truth.

It's my secret identity.

From the age of 4 all the way up to now, I've been reading Superman. If I weren't writing this book I could sit down today and write 50 sample scripts to submit to DC Comics.

So, of course, I have five things I learned from Superman:

A) I STILL AM SUPERMAN.

It wasn't just when I was 6. I have a secret identity disguised as the socially and physically awkward James Altucher that everyone sees but I know is not the real me.

Meanwhile, if everyone knew who I really was, they would be blown away by my powers. I know deep down how special I am. I'm originally from another planet, Krypton. Superman's Kryptonian name was Kal-El. Coincidentally, that is my Kryptonian name.

I'm misunderstood by the people of Earth. But I don't care. Everyday I wake up knowing I'm Superman and it makes me feel good.

B) SUPERMAN HAS NO USEFUL POWERS.

People always say Batman had no powers and Superman did. But it's actually the reverse.

Think about it: when would you ever need super strength? Are you really picking up a car anytime soon? No, of course not.

Heat vision? What for? I have a microwave.

X-ray vision? All of my neighbors are hideous even with clothes on. And we all know that women in general are sexier with skimpy clothes than totally naked.

And super hearing? I already know what everyone thinks about me. I think I would be horrified to hear them say those things.

What else? Oh yeah, flying. Where would you fly? And people would see you. And you'd eat flies and run into birds. Ewww. Forget it. I'm not flying. I don't even have a driver's license. I'll walk. Or take a train and watch a movie on my iPad.

Oh, and bullets don't affect Superman. To be honest, nobody has ever shot at me so this doesn't seem like a useful power to me.

But just knowing I'm Superman with secret powers is enough to make me happy. I AM Superman. I'm above the worries of Earthlings. And I believe that with everything inside of me. That's my secret. The secret has power.

C) EVERY DAY I WAKE UP AND SAY, "I AM GOING TO SAVE A LIFE."

All day long I look for situations where I can save a life. And I do it. Every day, I save at least one life.

Try it. Wake up tomorrow and say, "I'm going to save at least one life today." Even helping an old woman across the street counts. Even responding to an email and helping someone make an important decision saves a life. Even reaching out to a distant friend and asking how they're doing can save their life.

You can save a life today. Don't let the sun set without doing that.

You are Superman.

D) YOGA

Superman is the ultimate yogi. Not because of any flexibility. He's probably not very flexible actually because his joints and muscles are super tough. But he follows very well the basic precepts of yoga. He doesn't harm anyone, despite his capability of easily doing so. He doesn't lie (other than his secret identity, which he holds on to so others aren't harmed).

He's never possessive (why be possessive of anything if he can have anything he wants anytime he wants—like me). He practices "brahmacharya"—a form of celibacy or self-control, outside of his relationship with the beautiful Lois Lane. Even Napoleon Hill in his classic "Think and Grow Rich" has an entire chapter on this.

Superman also seems to have "santosha" (contentment). He never seems obsessed with grudges from his past. I've never seen him worry about his future.

I haven't always been Superman in this respect. But now I am. And NOW is all I care about.

E) ALL OF HIS FRIENDS ARE SUPERHEROES.

The Flash. Black Canary. Wonder Woman. Batman. Etc. They all have secret identities. They all see a world totally out of balance. They all have powers they use for good, that they use to bring balance back to the world.

All of my friends are superheroes also. Each one of my friends has a different power. But they are all amazing powers and I'm blessed when I see those powers in action. And once someone joins the bad guys, they are no longer my friend. I'm busy saving lives. I don't need bad friends.

I'm in my late 40s now. I no longer need to jump off a bed to prove I can fly. I know I'm going to save a life today. And nobody's going to figure out who I really am.

But I will tell you this. I'm Kal-El and I'm from the long dead planet Krypton.

7

SEVEN THINGS STAR WARS TAUGHT ME ABOUT PRODUCTIVITY

I saw the original "Star Wars" movie when I was 7 years old and it changed my life.

The series has had more influence on me than any other movie in history. I believe in the Force.

And I'm not the only one. In 2001, "Jedi" became the fourth most popular religion in the United Kingdom.

We all have faith in something—usually a mixture of some personal beliefs mixed with modern science. I am like that also. Mostly, I just believe in what works. Which, for me, is the Force. I admit it.

Here are some of the life lessons that I've learned from the Star Wars movies:

1) REST WHEN YOU HAVE NOTHING TO DO.

When Jedi Qui-Gon Jinn is fighting Darth Maul in "The Phantom Menace," a transparent door closes, dividing them. Darth Maul paces back and forth, ready to continue their battle while Qui-Gon simply sits and rests, seemingly doing nothing.

In modern society we all feel like we have to be Darth Maul. Pacing, finding a "purpose," being anxious, stressed, waiting for doors to open.

But it is great to just rest and be happy and not move when you don't have to. Those doors will open eventually.

2) RID YOURSELF OF EVERYTHING YOU DON'T NEED.

Obi-Wan lives a simple life in exile for 40 years when he's on

Tatooine. Yoda, Jedi master, lives in a simple swamp hut after he loses his battle with the Emperor.

They were still capable of laughing, of living, of staying healthy, and were able to train the next generation. They didn't need anything to keep them entertained.

It's a story. But this is the way I would like to live: with my friend and my health intact, and not a material care in the world.

3) PRACTICE GOODNESS.

Being a good, compassionate person is a quality we develop over years and thousands of hours of practice. Most people are not good people. In business, in art, in almost every "world" I've been in, most people I meet operate somewhere in the gray zone. A lot of times more toward the darker side of the spectrum.

It takes practice to be the person who is a source of compassion and honesty.

Supposedly it takes 10,000 hours to master something. Unfortunately, most people spend 10,000 hours trying to be jerks to others. If all you do is put in your 10,000 hours with small kindnesses, then the universe will return that many times over.

4) PRIORITIZE YOUR HEALTH.

In all of the movies, I never saw an out-of-shape Jedi. There seems to be a deep spiritual component to being a Jedi, but clearly there is a physical aspect as well. They are jumping out of spaceships, fighting with lightsabers, and they can probably run a four-minute mile. Heck, even Yoda at the age of 800 is jumping all over the place.

Health is important. If you are sick, then your thoughts will be stapled to that sickness. You can't get rid of it. You're in pain and pain takes up the mind and precludes you from doing the things you'd like to do.

This is why yoga is not about looking good in a yoga studio. It's about staying physically and emotionally healthy so you can focus on your spiritual life.

5) BE AROUND OTHER JEDIS.

Once Anakin Skywalker starts hanging out with Darth Sidious, he becomes a bad guy (see above).

Here are some things that are hard in life: being honest, being kind, and trying to add value to others. These things take time and energy. When you are around people who steal your energy, those things become even harder. As a wise man once said, "You are the average of the five people you spend the most time with."

6) BE OPEN-MINDED

This is a difference between Luke Skywalker and Han Solo in the original Star Wars.

Luke is willing to believe.

There are a lot of issues or ideas or beliefs people get "stapled to," almost as if they were sicknesses.

You'll probably at some point find yourself thinking that you know for SURE that you're on the RIGHT side of things.

But be willing to open your mind and look at why the other side thinks the way they do. It's never for the reasons you think.

Issues are just ways for the mind to practice being open-minded.

7) TRUST THAT LIFE IS CYCLICAL

Luke has to watch Obi-Wan die. Han has to be captured by bounty hunters. Anakin has to be recruited as a little kid. Qui-Gon has to die. Yoda has to go into exile. Bad things happen. But if you follow steps one through six, bad things happen in cycles. Good things also. Trusting that the kindness you are putting out there is compounding in a secret bank account for you means waiting for that bank account to deliver its returns. It will.

WHAT I'VE LEARNED
FROM ELON MUSK

C hoosing yourself means taking risks. It means not being afraid of what people think, or your chances of success vs. failure.

It means doing what you want and hopefully helping the world along the way.

Because when you help others, that's how you get paid in a *Choose Yourself* world.

Elon Musk is inspirational to many people, including me.

Inspiration is somewhat of a risk: it takes you outside of the world you once knew and introduces you to a new thought, person, idea, or something else totally unexpected.

I wanted to find Elon Musk's most inspirational quotes. The ones that might give clues to how each inspiration leads to the next. The ticking of the clock.

Here are his quotes that most stuck with me.

....

1. *"If something is important enough, even if the odds are against you, you should still do it."*

....

I often get stuck. What if something really is impossible?

But Elon Musk takes it to the next level always.

"Let's go to Mars."

Or, "Let's make a billion-dollar battery factory."

So at the very least it's always worth exploring the delicious curvature of the impossible.

2. *"Going from PayPal, I thought: 'Well, what are some of the other problems that are likely to most affect the future of humanity?' Not from the perspective, 'What's the best way to make money?'"*

I've interviewed hundreds of people now on my podcast. Each of them has achieved amazing results in their life.

That's a subjective opinion.

"Amazing" to me.

But none of them have done if for the money. I was talking to Coolio, for instance, who had the best-selling song of 1995.

He started writing lyrics every day in 1977. It took him 17 years to have a single hit.

"Never do something for the money," Coolio told me. "Or the girls," he added.

3. *"(Physics is) a good framework for thinking... Boil things down to their fundamental truths and reason up from there."*

My guess is he is not referring specifically to the science and theories of physics but the act of visualizing something, coming up with an idea or a theory of why it might be true, and then figuring out how to prove that theory.

To me, that's what physics is. Since the rules are constantly changing, which is another fascinating aspect of physics. Visualize a possible universe. Prove that it can happen.

....

4. *"The first step is to establish that something is possible; then probability will occur."*

....

I wonder about this. What's impossible? Maybe a time machine is too hard to figure out.

But to make an electric car you can imagine first a hybrid car that has a trunk filled with very efficient batteries so you don't ever need the gas part.

Then it becomes a function of probabilities versus possibilities.

....

5. *"It's OK to have your eggs in one basket as long as you control what happens to that basket."*

....

Many people think entrepreneurship is about risk. In fact, it's the opposite. Good entrepreneurs don't learn by failure (the popular "failure porn" all over the Internet).

Good entrepreneurs learn by solving difficult problems.

Elon Musk controlled his outcome with X.com not by destroying the competitor but by merging with it (PayPal).

6. *"Persistence is very important. You should not give up un-less you are forced to give up."*

I always think this is the magic equation: *persistence + love = abundance.*

You have to love something enough to persist. You have to persist enough to deepen your love.
This is true for a career. True for a relationship. But only true for YOU and not what someone tells you to do.

And then abundance is the natural outcome. Not just for you but for everyone. Since wealth comes to those who create wealth for others.

7. *"You want to have a future where you're expecting things to be better, not one where you're expecting things to be worse."*

This is incredibly important. News reporters have zero qualifications to inform people and yet they are all doom and gloom to sell subscriptions.

But people who choose themselves first imagine a better world and then imagine how to make the leap to get there.

8. *"It is a mistake to hire huge numbers of people to get a complicated job done. Numbers will never compensate for talent in getting the right answer (two people who don't know* *something are no better than one), will tend to slow down progress, and will make the task incredibly expensive."*

When I was running a software company, we always knew it would take one great programmer to solve a hard problem in one night versus 10 mediocre programmers taking a month to screw up a problem even worse.

Ultimately, if you want to make a TV show, don't rely on the gatekeepers.

Take a camera. Make a YouTube video. Make 100 YouTube videos. Now you have a show. All by yourself.

9. *"If you go back a few hundred years, what we take for granted today would seem like magic—being able to talk to people over long distances, to transmit images, flying, accessing vast amounts of data like an oracle. These are all things that would have been considered magic a few hundred years ago."*

And now imagine what it will be like 300 years from now when people look back at today. "They had to actually 'connect' to an Internet then!" or "It took them seven hours to get from NY to CA!"

10. *"[My biggest mistake is probably] weighing too much on someone's talent and not someone's personality. I think it matters whether someone has a good heart."*

I recently watched a company go from $1 billion in revenues to zero when a founder stole $90 million from the company. Integrity, humility, and doing your best are by far the most important considerations when evaluating whether to work for someone.

In order to choose yourself, you have to make sure you have completely surrounded yourself with others willing to take the same leaps. Else you will all fall into the ravine you are leaping over.

....

11. *"When I was in college, I wanted to be involved in things that would change the world."*

....

I always wonder about the phrase "change the world."

Perhaps the most valuable starting point is to do everything I can to change myself each day: to be physically healthier, to be around emotionally healthy people, to be create, to be grateful. To try and improve in these areas 1% a day.

Then maybe I can have a head start on changing the world.

....

12. *"I think it's very important to have a feedback loop, where you're constantly thinking about what you've done and how you could be doing it better. I think that's the single best piece of advice: constantly think about how you could be doing things better and questioning yourself."*

....

I'm invested in about 30 companies. The companies that fail are when CEOs smoke their own crack.

Technology, competition, customers are constantly changing. But we have a cognitive bias to think that the activity we have invested the most time in is, of course, a GREAT activity.

What could be wrong with it?

So it's important to constantly question this evolution-based cognitive bias with constant questioning, as if one were an outsider looking in. Without that, businesses fail.

And if you have trouble taking your own feedback, find someone you trust. Find an accountability partner. Ask, "Am I choosing myself?"

And when you find one, find a group. Have a meet-up of like-minded people.

Together is how we individually choose ourselves.

13. *"I wouldn't say I have a lack of fear. In fact, I'd like my fear emotion to be less because it's very distracting and fries my nervous system."*

A small level of fear is motivational. It forces me to have a backup plan. The average multimillionaire supposedly has seven sources of income. They all have backup plans.

Even Elon Musk has Tesla, SpaceX, SolarCity, and probably a dozen other companies he's peripherally involved in.

Any endeavor I do, I always ask two questions: "What is my plan B?" and "What is my evil plan?"

Meaning what do I hope to learn from this that nobody else expects?

---

14. *"Life is too short for long-term grudges."*

I always think that I'm the average of the five people I spend the most time with.

So this quote is important to me. Don't spend time with people who can even incite a grudge. I try to spend time with the people I love and who love me.

But even when something bad does happen, rather than blame, I try to think about what I learned. I don't want to make the same mistake again.

It takes practice. I am very trusting. But I hope to learn a little each day.

---

15. *"Don't be afraid of new arenas."*

Again, inspiration is a risk. It means stepping out of the comfort zone to somewhere you've never been before.

I try as an exercise to figure out at least one thing a day to do that is outside my comfort zone.

The other day I went up to people and asked them if I could buy a $1 bill with a $2 bill. Interestingly, everybody who was white avoided me. I was a lunatic. But everyone else took my $2 bill in exchange for a $1 bill.

You never know what you find when you experiment. But it's always fun and scary and good practice for getting out of the comfort zone.

---

16. *"I think it is possible for ordinary people to choose to be extraordinary."*

I thought about this when I read it. I think it's OK for "ordinary" people to be ordinary also. Ordinary is beautiful.

But I think every day it's worth trying to be a little better (even just 1%, an amount so small it can't be measured) in physical health, emotional health, creativity, and gratitude.

Maybe that is a path to extraordinary as that 1% compounds. But I don't want the pressure of "future extraordinary." I just want to be a little better today.

---

17. *"I could either watch it happen or be a part of it."*

Sometimes people say to me, "I missed the boat," or "I am too late." I think it's never too late to do what you love.
What you love is always on the shore, waiting for you to arrive, waiting with open arms.

---

18. *"Being an entrepreneur is like eating glass and staring into the abyss of death."*

People say to me, "I hate my cubicle. I want to be an entrepreneur."

Entrepreneurship is a disaster. About 85% of entrepreneurs fail and failure is not fun at all. Not to mention you have to deal with customers, employees, investors—they are all your bosses and not the other way around.

Then you have to sell, you have to execute, you have to build, you have to exit, you have to grow.

I like Elon Musk's approach of having many things to work on. Plans B and C and D and so on. So any one entrepreneurial endeavor doesn't take up all the mind space.

One secret, though, to beat that 85%. If you start off with a profitable customer, the odds of failure go from 85% to less than 20%.

19. *"I would like to die on Mars. Just not on impact."*

I highly recommend Andy Weir's book, *The Martian*. He self-published it. Then a major publisher picked it up. Then Ridley Scott made it into a movie.

20. *On his favorite book when he was a teen, The Hitchhiker's Guide to the Galaxy: "It taught me that the tough thing is figuring out what questions to ask, but that once you do that, the rest is really easy."*

Here's my favorite part of *The Hitchhiker's Guide to the Galaxy*: the idea that all you really need from a materialistic perspective is a towel.

Hygiene is key. Then the universe sort of takes care of things after that.

---

21. *"I just want to retire before I go senile because if I don't retire before I go senile, then I'll do more damage than good at that point."*

The two most critical years in terms of dying are the year you are born and the year you retire.

So I doubt Elon Musk will ever retire.

✳ ✳ ✳

Choosing yourself is not about launching a rocket to Mars. Or making $1 billion. Or even creating peace in the world.

It's about not letting anyone tell you that you can't.

It's about maneuvering around "can't," no matter what the risk.

It's about having a backup plan.

It's about health, to prepare you for the war against skeptics.

It's scary and exhilarating, and requires you to take action, and requires you to persist.

But it's worth it. Because nobody knows better than you what will set your life on fire and what will lift it into space and beyond.

6

SIX THINGS I LEARNED FROM MICK JAGGER

My kids don't know who the Rolling Stones are. They don't care either.

And why should they? Setting aside the common argument every generation makes with the generation after it ("our music is better than yours") what can distinguish Mick Jagger from, say, Selena Gomez, whom they admire? Or Adele? Or any of the other musicians that they could listen to all day long (after covering their ears if I play any music from the '60s, '70s, '80s, or '90s).

Here's what I get curious about:

* *How did the band survive for 50 years?* Same front man: Mick Jagger. Same guy on guitar: Keith Richards. Same guy on drums: Charlie Watts. Drugs, divorces, deaths, diseases, debt—they just kept going.
* *Unlike their peers:* The Beatles, the Doors, Jimi Hendrix, Pink Floyd, Led Zeppelin. How do they keep going? What made them different? They don't even like each other that much if you believe the ramblings in Keith Richards' autobiography, "Life." It's hard to like people for 50 years straight. I have a hard time being around the same people for 24 hours, let alone 50 years.
* *How did they succeed?* And create? What made them stand out? So many times you hear a young band and they just sound like every other band. Nothing unique. Nothing that makes you want to say, "In 50 years, I'm still going to be listening to them."

A) OBSESSION WITH MUSIC

They all met and bonded because they were obsessed not with

rock (Elvis, The Beatles, etc.) but with the blues (Chuck Berry, Muddy Waters, Bo Diddley, etc.). The band's name comes from the song "Rollin' Stone" written by Muddy Waters.

In fact, almost all of their initial songs, performances, and initial song releases were all covers of Chicago blues bands. Their first hit to get into the top 10 for instance was a cover of a Buddy Holly song.

But it's an obsession with the history of music that brought them together. Richards and Jagger, childhood friends who lost touch, ran into each other at a bus stop when they were about 18 and Jagger was carrying a Chuck Berry record. Richards recognized a kindred spirit and they were inseparable after that.

B) BLUES MEETS ROCK

They didn't remain just blues. In fact, they were like the Borg and kept assimilating every musical style that came after them.

Someone once asked me whether it was better to be good at a lot of things or GREAT at one thing.

The answer is exemplified by the Rolling Stones. They were "good" at EVERY style of music and thus became the GREATEST at the intersection of all of those styles. While The Beatles combined pop/Elvis/early rock, the Rolling Stones covered those forms plus blues and R&B (and Jagger's leg motions certainly had an Elvis influence. The band even had a strong Beatles influence).

Things like this remind me of Bobby Fischer and chess. When he was kid he was considered a talented young chess player but certainly not the best ever. Not even the best young player ever. So he did what he normally did when he needed to take a step up. He disappeared.

He did a comprehensive study of all the games played in the 1800s. This was around the age of 13. When he returned to play, he would play these "old fashioned" openings from the 1850s but he'd throw in his own subtle improvements that he had developed.

Within a year or so, he was U.S. Champion and on his way to being World Champion (after disappearing again and learning Russian so he could read all the Russian chess magazines).

I think of the bands that stand out for me now. I was just listening to Gotan Project, which combines old school tango music with a more techno feel. Or creators like Steve Jobs who so effectively combined design with technology (not only with Apple but with Pixar) in ways that had never been done before.

It's hard to be the greatest at any one endeavor, but by combining passions, it's much easier to be the greatest in the world at the intersections of those passions (because there are billions of things that can intersect, you can find your own place in the "long tail of passion" to be the master of).

It's hard to call "Sympathy for the Devil" or "Paint It Black" rock, or blues, or any other musical style. The only way to describe it is that it's the musical style that the Stones defined by carving out the intersection of several styles.

It's worth noting that even though they continued to assimilate future styles in the decades to come, it's these initial songs (and several others) that they wrote in the '60s and early '70s that continue to be played over and over again—the results of their initial passions and first loves.

It's also interesting that Jagger not only found himself the greatest at various intersections of music but also literature. After reading Mikhail Bulgakov's novel "The Master and the Margarita," which had the line of Satan being "a man of wealth and taste," Jagger wrote the lyrics for "Sympathy for the Devil."

C) PERSISTENCE/REJECTION

The band was constantly rejected. Their initial songs didn't make the top charts. Their record label, Decca, did zero promotion for their first release.

And reviewers couldn't stand Jagger's voice.

"Very ordinary. I can't hear a word Jagger's saying," said one reviewer.

"Fuzzy and undisciplined…complete chaos," said another.

Also he couldn't play any instruments (at that time). So they simply weren't the best band out there.

But they kept playing. They also had the extra quality of Jagger's charisma, which seemed above and beyond the talent of the band by itself.

At the time, the band was "run" by Brian Jones, who was the first person to eventually quit the band (in 1969) and basically the last person of the original guys to quit (well, 35 years later Bill Wyman retired, but Jagger, Watts, Richards are all from the original band).

Given that Jones was running things, it took awhile for the Rolling Stones to realize that Jagger was the attraction. Nevertheless, they didn't let rejection stop them. It was several years of playing before they started hitting the charts and several more before they were touring and making good money.

My theory always in any career is that it takes one to three years to do the studying required. About two years before you are making any money at the new career. Three to four years before you are making a living from it and five to six years before you are killing it.

But it requires persistence each day.

D) ARTISTS GROWING UP TOGETHER

I'm always amazed at how groups of artists, businessmen, creators of any sort, basically grow up together in their respective businesses. In writing, look at Jack Kerouac, Allen Ginsberg, William S. Burroughs, all hanging out together years before any of their books reached any kind of acclaim.

Or Steve Jobs and Bill Gates. Or in the art world, Jasper Johns, John Cage, Robert Rauschenberg, all living on basically the same block in downtown New York, exploring the art scene of the '50s.

It was no different for the Rolling Stones. There was one concert where lack of any money forced them all to hitch rides together with young musicians Jimmy Page (Led Zeppelin), Eric Clapton, etc. on the way to see The Beatles in concert.

One time, Jagger and Richards decided they needed to start writing their own music. They had no idea where to start. They simply couldn't write music. So Andrew Oldham was wandering around outside and ran into Paul McCartney and John Lennon and explained the problem.

Lennon and McCartney went up to the apartment Jagger and Richards shared and basically riffed out "I Wanna Be Your Man" to help the Stones put together the release that was their first major hit.

E) NEVER SAY NO

The Stones said yes to everything. They would perform 200 places a year for almost no money in the beginning. The just kept saying "yes," even if it meant playing to crowds of just four or five people.

This reminds me of when The Beatles were playing almost 20 hours a day, seven days a week at strip clubs in Hamburg, West Germany from 1960 to 1962. It was the non-stop playing that gave them experience and mastery.

Malcolm Gladwell refers to this in his excellent book "Outliers" as the time when the Beatles got their 10,000 hours in order to achieve mastery before they hit it big.

For early entrepreneurs, this can translate to saying "yes" to every networking opportunity, every meeting that can result in down-the-road potential for customers, investors, acquirers, and great future employees.

Most meetings are complete wastes of time. But I think it takes going to lots of meetings to build the bullshit detector to determine what is a waste of time and what isn't.

That said, you can still learn from 100% of the meetings. Sergey Brin, for instance, used to interview every potential Google employee. He explained later that he knew within seconds whether he would hire someone and would then spend the rest of the meeting trying to learn at least one new thing from the interviewee so the meeting wouldn't be a total waste of time.

With Jagger, the ability to say "yes" to everything also translated to the inability to say "no" to anything. He originally felt he would retire from the Stones when he was 33.

"I couldn't bear to end up as an Elvis Presley... and sing to all those old ladies coming in with their handbags."

Well, now he's 73 and is still playing.

It is this that ultimately held the group together—the band members' loyalty to nothing (family, friends, other art pursuits) other than the band.

They were addicts but the biggest addiction they had was adulation to this entity they created. For better or worse, since it made them all an enormous amount of money.

F) CONTENT IS JUST THE TRUNK OF A TREE

Then there are a 1,000 branches. People all the time ask me how you make money from writing a blog. Or writing a book.

There really is no way. Most authors will tell you the fastest way to go broke is to spend years writing a book. Same goes for blogs.

But you use the content you create as a launching pad. In the case of blogs—speaking gigs, consulting gigs, multiple books, subscription products, etc. I've seen some bloggers make millions not off of their blogs but off of the ancillary activities that happened because they built up their platform through blogging, tweeting, Facebook, etc.

The Stones are no different. They don't even own most of their successful music. Like many musicians from the '60s or earlier, they mistakenly signed away all of the rights to their music without even realizing it. The rights to the songs you know—"Paint It Black," "Sympathy," "Satisfaction," "You Can't Always Get What You Want," and on and on—were signed away to their manager Allen Klein.

So they don't make any money off of those. And how many people can name Stones' songs written in the '80s? I can't. (Well, "State of Shock," which Mick Jagger did with Michael Jackson. But that's it.)

SO HOW DID THEY MAKE ANY MONEY?

Tours. They made over $600 million on their last tour. They form a company at the beginning of each tour and collect all the revenues of the tour, including sponsorships, tickets, clothing, record sales, etc. (thanks to Jagger's businesslike abilities acquired from attending the London School of Economics before the band started). Then they divide out the proceeds at the end of the tour, all taking home a nice paycheck. Jagger was analytical on every aspect of the business, even inquiring with managers about which currency would be stronger, the pound or the dollar, over time.

They've done over 40 tours, with four of their tours appearing in the list of top 10 grossing tours of all time. Interesting to note that Lady Gaga's most successful tour grossed "only" $234 million, but it can be argued she didn't have to split it as many ways and still has a long career ahead of her.

By the way, for my friends who write non-fiction books: I've seen people write best sellers to non-sellers, but the ONLY way that I've seen serious money being made by authors that I know (even for the bestsellers) is by either doing speaking tours after the book comes out (far exceeding whatever they got in advances) or by selling information products that complement the value they deliver in their books.

The Rolling Stones is not my favorite band. Some of their songs are among my favorites but I've never bought an album and I don't think I've ever bought any of their songs. I've never seen them on tour. I barely know anything about them. But I'm fascinated by their longevity, the birth of their creativity, the glue that stuck them together and propelled them from despair to success, and ultimately the magic of creativity that infects anyone who reaches the status they reached. I hope one day in my own way to achieve a tiny sliver of that.

IS POPE FRANCIS AN ATHEIST? (AND 10 OTHER THINGS I LEARNED FROM HIM)

M y grandparents were disgusted with me when my first three girlfriends were all Catholics.

"What do they cook?" my grandmother asked. (Cooking, of course, being the great differentiator in religion.)

She even said, "Goulash?" Like it was a curse.

Many years later, after a lot of grief, I sat in St. Patrick's in N.Y.C., praying for money.

"Please God, make my life better by giving me money."

It didn't matter to me that it was a church. I was so scared I didn't know what to do.

I would do anything, even pray to a god I didn't believe in, in a house of worship that I didn't feel welcome in, and asking for something that prayer was never intended for.

Someone asked me yesterday, "What do you feel strongly about?"

I said, "Nothing."

He said, "That's a strong response. Don't you worry about death?"

I said, "Why waste any part of today worrying about something that will happen later?"

Today Pope Francis arrives at St. Patrick's in N.Y.C. My guess is his motives will be loftier than mine. But I don't know. Maybe he wants money also.

So I did some research. God or not, religion or not, Catholic or not, I try to learn from everyone.

Here's what I learned from (and loved about) Pope Francis:

A) HE LIVES IN A STUDIO

When Pope Francis traveled to the Vatican for his inauguration he stayed in a hotel that he paid for himself.

And rather than move into the lavish 12-bedroom residence all prior popes live in, he chose a small studio with no staff.

Rather than mimic him, it's interesting to just ask "why?" and think about it.

What is the example he wants to live by?

B) CUBA

Pope Francis wrote letters to Barack Obama and Raúl Castro, encouraging them to get together.

That's why we have relations once again with Cuba, after 50 years.

Biologically we're one species. But politically, for thousands of years we've divided ourselves up with false and artificial borders.

Imagine a world with no borders. Where trade and innovation flourish. Where friendship and kindness can transcend ethnic and religious differences.

A world with no more arguing on daytime talk shows.

C) HE TOOK A SELFIE

A bunch of teenagers approached him and asked him for a photo. They took a selfie.

He doesn't put himself on a pedestal (he drives a Kia instead of the previous "pope-mobile"). He wants to show that we all have the potential for direct happiness.

During the time of Jesus, there was no pope obviously.

In fact, Jesus said, "The kingdom of God is within you."

And that's why the Pope takes a selfie.

He said, "Depicting the pope as a sort of Superman, a star, is offensive to me. The pope is a man who laughs, cries, sleeps calmly and has friends like everyone else. A normal person."

D) HE MAKES PHONE CALLS

Two years ago, a young woman was pressured by her husband to have an abortion.

She said "no" and got divorced.

She was depressed. She wrote the pope.

A few weeks later the phone rang. She picked it up.

"Hello," the other side said. "It's Pope Francis." He comforted her and then baptized the newborn when it was born.

He regularly makes calls to the people who write him, shedding the layers of bureaucracy that have existed for almost 2,000 years in the Vatican.

How often we forget the immense benefits a simple touch makes.

The most impressive display of beauty is not the Sistine Chapel, with God reaching to grasp the first man... but a man reaching out to touch a single woman who needed help.

How many of us do that simple act, the creation of art and beauty, every day? I don't.

But I should.

D) HE HATES THE NEWS

"The media only writes about the sinners and the scandals, but that's normal, because a tree that falls makes more noise than a forest that grows."

The media sells subscriptions. But every day we have a choice. To focus on what is growing in our lives, or the negativity and fear that try to bring us down.

Another quote: "How can it be that it is not a news item when an elderly homeless person dies of exposure but it is news when the stock market loses two points?"

E) THE INSIGNIFICANCE OF MAN

There are somewhere around eight million species on Earth. We always think of ourselves as somehow "king" of the food chain.

Maybe we are and maybe we aren't. After all, we made the definition of the phrase "food chain" so why not make ourselves king of it.

Certainly many species are not even aware of us.

Nor is it so great that we are supposedly "intelligent." How many high IQ people are truly happy and free and live every day with well-being?

Francis's quote: "No one can grow if he does not accept his smallness."

F) HE TEACHES PEOPLE TO CHOOSE THEMSELVES

We know that happiness is not related to money. Countless studies have shown this.

Often it's related to our mindset. To the choices we make. Again, when someone asked me why not worry about tomorrow, there is no real answer. Why should I?

Another Pope Francis quote: "This is the struggle of every person: be free or be a slave."

Even if you are stuck at the bottom of solitary confinement in jail, you can still choose to be free inside your spirit.

This is not self-help B.S. This is your choice: do you be miserable or do you root yourself in your inner freedom? Why choose to be miserable?

And yet, often when I wake up in the morning, all my past memories suck me in as quickly as possible and it's an effort not to say "ugh."

Then I'm a slave again. It's a practice every day to choose freedom.

G) HE SECRETLY READS MY EMAILS

His quote: "Living together is an art. It's a patient art, it's a beautiful art, it's fascinating."

Do you ever feel like that? Like you argue with someone and the only way out of it is to crawl into a cave. To disappear and not even think until the storm seems to pass.
But it does pass. And you figure your way through the maze to find a greater intimacy.

I don't brag about it. I hate arguing. I don't ever want to. I'd honestly rather have less intimacy in my life than argue to find greater intimacy.

But when it's there I do feel like I just helped to make a work of art.

H) HE DOESN'T TEACH FEAR

For all I know, he is an atheist. I can't find one quote from him about hell or damnation.

In my view (and I may be wrong, it doesn't matter to me) he uses the word "God" as a placeholder for "well-being."

Many studies show that the key to contentment and confidence is three things:

* Growing competence in a pursuit you love
* Strengthening every day the relationships around you
* Increasing your freedom of choices

Quote from the pope: "If we start without confidence, already we have lost half the battle and we bury our talents."

I) HE THINKS LIKE THE DALAI LAMA

A friend of mine who is a believer in Tibetan Buddhism and has spent much time with the Dalai Lama once said to me: "When you are with the Dalai Lama, you feel as if he loves you the way a mother loves her baby."

Quote from Francis: "To protect every man and every woman, to look upon them with tenderness and love, is to open up a horizon of hope. It is to let a shaft of light break through the heavy clouds; it is to bring the warmth of hope!"

J) LIVE BY EXAMPLE INSTEAD OF PREACHING

Imagine you've had a hard day at your construction site. You finally get a break, sit down with your friends, and break out your lunch.

A man walks by. He's also tired from his job. He leaves the crowd surrounding him and asks you and your friends if he can join you for lunch.

He pulls out his lunchbox also and starts eating and talking to you.

He lives in a simple studio, drives a simple car, and refuses all gifts anyone gives him.

He's the pope. And this happened.

Quote: "These two criteria are like the pillars of true love: deeds, and the gift of self."

He doesn't just say it. He lives it.

It doesn't matter if you are Jewish. It doesn't matter if you are an atheist. It doesn't matter if you are Christian, or Catholic.

Pope Francis lives a message. I wish every day I could try to live closer to that same message.

K) HIS NAME IS HIS ENTIRE BELIEF SYSTEM

He chose the name Francis when he became pope because of Francis of Assisi. Why?

He explains:

"Francis of Assisi loved, helped and served the needy, the sick and the poor; he also cared greatly for creation."

To me, this is the entire belief system of Pope Francis. He did not use the words "God" or "Jesus" or "spirit" above.

This is all anyone needs to transform a life of fear and stress and anxiety and regret into a life of well-being and happiness.

Sometimes I think I'm not a good person. Sometimes I look at people on the street and hate them for no reason. Sometimes I'm not as good as I could be to family or friends.

But I'm trying to be better. I hope every day I can wake up and remind myself of Francis's exact words above.

"To care greatly for creation" is the essence of choosing yourself instead of letting anyone else do it for you.

Instead of being held back by judgments or anger or fear or regret.

Maybe one day I will be able to live in a studio, call people who need help, eat lunch with strangers, take selfies with whomever.

For now, I'll write this book.

FIVE THINGS I
LEARNED FROM
GANDHI

irst, two small stories:

STORY #1: A woman walks with her son many miles and for many days to come to see Gandhi. She is very worried about her son's health because he is eating too much sugar. She comes to Gandhi and says, "Please, sir, can you tell my son to stop eating sugar?"

Gandhi looks at her and thinks for a bit and finally says, "OK, but not today. Bring him back in two weeks."

She's disappointed and takes her son home. Two weeks later, she makes the journey again and goes to Gandhi with her son.

Gandhi says to the boy, "You must stop eating sugar. It's very bad for you."

The boy has such respect for Gandhi that he stops and lives a healthy life.

The woman is confused and asks him, "Gandhi, please tell me, why did you want me to wait two weeks to bring back my son?"

Gandhi said, "Because before I could tell your son to stop eating sugar, I had to stop eating sugar first."

STORY #2: One of Gandhi's financial backers once said, "It's very expensive to keep Gandhi in poverty."

I suspect the financial backers felt they had some influence on Gandhi. But money means nothing to a spiritual leader.

One time, Gandhi said to a group of his backers, "I need to set aside one hour a day for meditation."

One of the backers said, "Oh no, you can't do that! You are too busy, Gandhi!"

Gandhi said, "Well, then, I now need to set aside two hours a day for meditation."

Five lessons from this:

1. *Nobody can tell you what to do.* No matter what they pay you. No matter what obligations you feel you owe them. Every second defines you. Be who you are, not who anyone else is. An entrepreneur, for instance, has investors, customers, partners, employees, competitors. Everyone wants their inputs heard. But only you can act to change the world with your ideas.

2. *If he was, in fact too busy,* then it meant he was not devoting enough time to his spiritual life. Hence his backer inadvertently convinced him he needed two hours a day to devote to silence and contemplation. It is through silence that sound, activity, action erupt. It was through nothingness that the Big Bang, and all subsequent creation, erupted. It is only through contemplation that the hidden shades of reality can be seen and right action can be taken. Gandhi knew this, and single-handedly brought down an empire. It's only through stillness that one can be creative.

3. *I don't give any advice* on things I don't know about first hand. Sometimes I find myself in a political conversation and I realize, "You know what? I don't actually know anything here." And I give up. Or when a reader sends me a question, I only send a response back that I have personally experienced or seen the advice I am recommending.

4. *Sugar is bad.* And since most processed carbs break down into sugar, it's all bad for you if you want to live a healthy life. Almost every disease out there comes from extra weight. The extra weight comes from the sugars that the body breaks down so quickly it forgets to digest.

5. *Nothing is more important than the cultivation* of yourself. So many people think they will save the world if they defeat "them," where "them" is some evil force that is bringing the world down.

But once you divide the world into categories, into an "us" versus "them," then you immediately become the "them" and you lose touch with who you really are.

Society is made up of individuals. The only way to improve society is to come at it from a place of deep satisfaction. The only way to do that is to spend long periods of time just being silent.

Ask yourself, "What is generating these thoughts?" in order to find the real you. They are not your thoughts. That is just the biological brain dancing in front of you. Who is the "you" they are dancing in front of? Then you can save the world.

Gandhi knew he could only be effective if he identified with the real "me," which was deeper than the body named "Gandhi" that was supposedly saving the world. The world is filled with strife. India is a mess now, regardless of what Gandhi did. But Gandhi provided a beacon while he lived.

Both of these stories are about the same thing, even though they seem completely different. You've probably heard the Gandhi quote, "Be the change you wish to see in the world." The truth is he didn't say exactly that. What he said was:

> *"We but mirror the world. All the tendencies present in the outer world are to be found in the world of our body. If we could change ourselves, the tendencies in the world would also change. As a man changes his own nature, so does the attitude of the world change towards him. This is the divine mystery supreme. A wonderful thing it is and the source of our happiness. We need not wait to see what others do."*

Every day I try hard to live by that quote. I hope you can also.

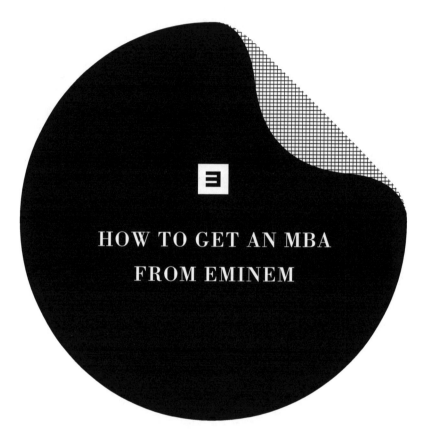

HOW TO GET AN MBA
FROM EMINEM

In 2002, I was driving to a hedge fund manager's house hoping to raise money from him. I was two hours late. This was pre-GPS and I had no cell phone. I was totally lost. If you've never driven around Connecticut you need to know one thing: all the roads are parallel and they all have the same name. And all the towns have the same name.

I know that doesn't make sense. But drive in that state and you will see what I mean. Also, their computers don't work. For the life of me, I can't figure out how to get rid of my outstanding driving violations in Connecticut.

I was two hours late and I kept playing "Lose Yourself" by Eminem over and over again. Maybe this was subconsciously making me "lose myself," I don't know.

But I kept thinking I had one shot and I was going to blow it by not showing up.

Finally I got there. The hedge fund manager was dressed all in pink. His house was enormous. Maybe 20,000 square feet. His cook served us a great meal. I had made him wait two hours to eat. And he had cancer at the time. I felt really bad.

Then we played chess and it was fun and he gave me a tour of the house. One room was just for toys made in 1848. He had a squash court inside the house. Another room had weird artifacts, like the handwritten notes when Lennon and McCartney were first writing down the lyrics for "Hey Jude." Another was the official signed statement by Ted Kennedy in the police station after he reported the Chappaquiddick incident that ultimately caused him to never be president.

Eventually I did raise money and it started a new life for me.

But that's not why I bring up Eminem at all.

The song "Lose Yourself" is from the movie "8 Mile." Although I recommend it, you don't have to see it to understand what I am about to write. I'll give you everything you need to know.

Eminem is a genius at sales and competition and he shows it in one scene in the movie. A scene I will break down for you line by line so you will know everything there is to know about sales, cognitive bias, and defeating your competition.

First, here's all you need to know about the movie.

Eminem is a poor, no-collar, white trash guy living in a trailer park. He's beaten on, works crappy jobs, gets betrayed, etc. But he lives to rap and break out somehow.
In the first scene he is having a "battle" against another rapper and he chokes. He gives up without saying a word. He's known throughout the movie as someone who chokes under pressure and he seems doomed for failure.

Until he chooses himself.

The scene I will show you and then break down is the final battle in the movie. He's the only white guy and the entire audience is black. He's up against the reigning champion that the audience loves.

He wins the battle and I will show you how, with his techniques, you can go up against any competition.

After he wins it, he can go on to do anything he wants. Win any battles. Even run the battles each week. But he walks off because he's going to do his own thing. He chooses himself. The movie is autobiographical. And 300 million records later he is the most successful rapper in history.

OK, let's break it down. How did Eminem win so easily?

Setting aside his talent for a moment (let's assume both sides are equally talented), Eminem used a series of cognitive biases to win the battle.

The current human brain was developed over 400,000 years ago. In fact, arguably, when the brain was used more to survive in nomadic situations, humans had higher IQs then they have today. But one very important thing is that the brain developed many biases as sort of short-cuts to survival.

For instance, a very common one is that we have a bias toward noticing negative news over positive news. The reason is simple: if you were in the jungle and you saw a lion to your right and an apple tree to your left, you would best ignore the apple tree and run as fast as possible away from the lion. This is called "negativity bias" and it's the entire reason newspapers still survive—by very explicitly exploiting this bias in humans.

We no longer need those shortcuts as much. There aren't that many lions in the street. But the brain took 400,000 years to evolve and it's only in the past 50 years maybe that we are relatively safe from most of the dangers that threatened earlier humans. Our technology and ideas have evolved but our brains can't evolve fast enough to keep up with them.

Consequently, these biases are used in almost every sales campaign, business, marketing campaign, movie, news piece, relationship, everything. Almost all of your interactions are dominated by biases and understanding them is helpful when calling B.S. on your thoughts.

Your brain loves and wants to protect you. But it's not smart enough because life has evolved faster than the brain. So you have to learn how to reach past the signals from the brain and develop intuition and mastery over these biases.

1) "IN GROUP" BIAS

Notice Eminem's first line: "Now everybody from the 313, put your mother****ing hands up and follow me."

The number 313 is the area code for Detroit. And not just Detroit. It's for blue collar, black Detroit where the entire audience, and Eminem, is from. So he wipes away the "out group" bias that might be associated with his race and he changes the conversation to "who is in 313 and who is NOT in 313."

2) HERD BEHAVIOR

He said, "Put your hands up and follow me." Everyone starts putting their hands up without thinking. So their brain tells them that they are doing this for rational reasons. For instance, they are now following Eminem.

3) AVAILABILITY CASCADE

The brain has a tendency to believe things even more if they are repeated, regardless of whether or not they are true. This is called an "availability cascade." There is a cascade of information that is available to you and it's all the same, so you feel the need to believe it. It must be true.

Notice Eminem repeats his first line. After he does that he no longer needs to say, "Follow me." He says, "Look, look." They are already following him and under his command. So he says, "look," because he is about to point out the enemy. He is setting up the next cognitive bias.

4) DISTINCTION BIAS OR "OUT GROUP" BIAS

Brains have a tendency to view two things as very different if they are evaluated at the same time as opposed to evaluated separately. Eminem wants his opponent, Papa Doc, to be evaluated right then as someone different from the group, even though the reality is they are all in the same group of friends with similar interests, etc.

Eminem says, "Now while he stands tough, notice that this man did not have his hands up."

In other words, even though Papa Doc is black, like everyone in the audience, he is no longer "in the group" that Eminem has defined and commanded: the 313 group. He has completely changed the conversation from race to area code.

5) AMBIGUITY BIAS

He doesn't refer to Papa Doc by name. He says "this man." In other words, there's "the 313 group" which we are all a part of in the audience, and now there is this ambiguous man who is attempting to invade us.

Watch presidential campaign debates. A candidate will rarely refer to another candidate by name. Instead, he might say, "My opponent might think X, but we here know that Y is better."

When the brain starts to view a person with ambiguity it gets confused and can't make choices involving that ambiguity. So the person without ambiguity wins.

6) CREDENTIAL BIAS

Because the brain wants to take short cuts, it will look for information more often from people with credentials or lineage than from people who come out of nowhere.

So, for instance, if one person was from Harvard and told you it was going to rain today and another random person told you it was going to be sunny today, you might be more inclined to believe the person from Harvard.

Eminem does this subtly two lines later. He says, "One, two, three, and to the four."

This is a direct line from Snoop Dogg's first song with Dr. Dre, "Nuthin' But a G Thang." It is the first line in the song and perhaps one of the most well-known rap lines ever. Outside of the context of the movie, Eminem was actually discovered by Dr. Dre. There's an interesting lineage of: N.W.A., Dr. Dre, Eminem, and 50 Cent. The most popular rappers ever.

But in this battle, Eminem directly associates himself with well-known successful rappers Dr. Dre and Snoop when he uses that line.

He then use the availability cascade again by saying, "One Pac, two Pac, three Pac, four." First, he's using that line "one, two, three, and to the four" again, but this time with Pac, which refers to the rapper Tupac. So now he's associated himself in this little battle in Detroit with three of the greatest rappers ever.

7) IN GROUP/OUT GROUP

Eminem points to random people in the audience and says, "You're Pac, he's Pac," including them with him in associating their lineages with these great rappers. But then he points to his opponent, Papa Doc, makes a gesture like his head is being sliced off and says, "You're Pac, NONE." Meaning that Papa Doc has no lineage, no credibility, unlike Eminem and the audience.

8) BASIC DIRECT MARKETING: LIST THE OBJECTIONS UP FRONT

Any direct marketer or salesperson knows the next technique Eminem uses. When you are selling a product, or yourself, the person or group you are selling to is going to have easy objections. They know those objections and you know those objections. If you don't bring them up and they don't bring them up then they will not buy your product. If they bring it up before you, then it looks like you were hiding something and you just wasted a little of their time by forcing them to bring it up.

So a great sales technique is to address all of the objections in advance.

Eminem's next set of lines does this brilliantly.

He says, "I know everything he's got to say against me."

And then he just lists them one by one:

> *"I am white, I am a fuckin' bum;*
> *I do live in a trailer with my mom;*
> *My boy Future is an Uncle Tom;*
> *I do got a dumb friend named Cheddar Bob*
> *Who shoots himself in the leg with his own gun;*
> *I did get jumped by all six of you chumps."*

And so on. He lists several more. But at the end of the list, there's no more criticism you can make of him. He's addressed everything and dismissed them.

In a rap battle (or a sales pitch), if you address everything your opponent can say, he's left with nothing to say. When he has nothing to say, the audience, or the sales prospect, will buy from you.

Look at direct marketing letters you get in email. They all spend pages and pages addressing your concerns. This is one of the most important techniques in direct marketing.

9) HUMOR BIAS

Eminem saves his best for last.

"But I know something about you," he says while staring at Papa Doc.

He sings it playfully, making it stand out and almost humorous. There is something called humor bias. People remember things that are stated humorously more than they remember serious things.

10) EXTREME OUT GROUP

"You went to Cranbrook."

And then Eminem turns to his "313 group" for emphasis as he explains what Cranbrook is.

"That's a private school."

BAM! There's no way now the audience can be on Papa Doc's side but Eminem makes the out group even larger.

"His real name's Clarence…And Clarence's parents have a real good marriage."

BAM and BAM! Two more things that separate Papa Doc from the crowd. He's a nerdy guy who goes to a rich school, and his parents are together. Unlike probably everyone in the audience, including Eminem. No wonder Papa Doc doesn't live in the 313.

11) CREDENTIAL BIAS (AGAIN)

Eminem says, "'Cause here no such things as…" and the audience chants with him:

"Halfway crooks!"

Because they know exactly what he is quoting: a line from a song by Mobb Deep, another huge East Coast rap group (so now Eminem has established lineage between himself and both the West Coast and the East Coast).

And by using the audience to say "halfway crooks," they're all in the same group again while Clarence goes back to his home with his parents at the end of the show.

12) SCARCITY

The music stops, which means Eminem has to stop and let Papa Doc have his turn.

But he doesn't. He basically says, "F*ck everybody, f*ck y'all if you doubt me. I don't wanna win. I'm outie."

He makes himself scarce. After establishing total credibility with the audience he basically says he doesn't want what they have to offer. He reduces the supply of himself by saying he's out of there. Maybe he will never come back. Reduce the supply of yourself while demand is going up and what happens? Basic economics.

Value goes up.

He's so thoroughly dominated the battle that now, in reversal to the beginning of the movie, Papa Doc chokes. He doesn't quite choke, though. There's nothing left to say. Eminem has said it all for him. There's no way Papa Doc can raise any "objections" because Eminem has already addressed them all. All he can do is defend himself, which will give him the appearance of being weak. And he's so thoroughly not in the 313 group that there is no way to get back in there.

There's simply nothing left to say. So Eminem wins the battle.

And what does Eminem do with his victory? He can do anything.

But he walks away from the entire subculture. He walks off at the end of the movie with no connection to what he fought for.

He's going to choose himself to be successful and not rely on the small-time thinking in battles in Detroit.

He's sold 220 million records worldwide. He discovered and produced 50 Cent, who has sold hundreds of millions more (and is another example of "Choose Yourself" as Robert Greene so aptly describes in his book, "The 50th Law").

Doesn't it seem silly to analyze a rap song for ideas how to be better at sales and communicating? I don't know. You tell me.

NINE THINGS I LEARNED
from
SERENA WILLIAMS

I think I love Serena Williams. I mean, she hasn't returned any of my emails or countless phone calls but I feel there is a connection. I see her on TV and I feel like there's a spark.

Maybe I just want to be her for a day.

What if we could do that? Just agree to switch places with people all day long. And we can never return to the same body twice. I think I just solved war and poverty with that idea. I hope someone invents this.

If there is anything I've consistently studied in life, it's what it takes to master any field.

One thing I know for sure: talent helps, but it can also hurt.

About 20 years ago I knew an 11-year-old kid who, at that time, was probably one of the best chess players in the world.

I never saw someone so talented. He could destroy grandmasters at blitz chess. At age 12. I was really jealous of him. I was a 27-year-old failure and he was at the beginning of magic.

In every other way he was a little kid but when he was analyzing chess games it was like speaking to the most mature adult I'll ever speak to.

Then…he disappeared. He stopped playing.

I asked around why. He couldn't handle losing at all. His talent convinced him he should always be better than everyone else. One loss and his view of himself was crushed. Talent had destroyed him.

Talent is the tiniest of sparks. A spark lights the fire. But you have to feed the fire more fuel to keep it going. Else it dies out.

How many of us have had that spark? And then years of being beaten down have put out the fire?

Me!

Being beaten down and asking, "Why is this happening AGAIN?!"

Serena Williams is the perfect example of someone who has talent, but also worked for 30 years at honing that talent into a skill.

If she had never worked at that talent, she would be a mediocre tennis player at best.

When she was 3 years old, her dad gave Serena her very first tennis racket.

He homeschooled her. He moved to Florida where they could practice tennis year-round. He coached her every day in tennis and had her playing in the junior circuit before she was 10 years old.

She's 35 now. She's the best female tennis player of all time.

When you get a chance to view someone who is the best out of seven billion people at something, you get a tiny glimpse at the potential of the human species.

The top 1% means you are in the top 70 million people. That seems doable.

That's why I like to listen to what Serena Williams has to say. What has she seen? What has she felt? What does she know?

Because now I want to know. A glimpse of the world using Serena's eyes.

Here are some quotes from Serena that I've learned from:

A) LUCK

"Luck has nothing to do with it, because I have spent many, many hours, countless hours, on the court working for my one moment in time, not knowing when it would come."

We often daydream, and think, and plan.

But the only thing that gets results is action. Not a single ounce of greatness in history ended with thoughts. It happened with hands. With actions.

B) SATISFACTION

"I can't become satisfied, because if I get satisfied, I'll be like, 'Oh, I've won Wimbledon, I've won the U.S. Open. Now can I relax.' But now people are really going to be fighting to beat me."

When I sold my first business I automatically assumed I was this amazing genius.

So I started throwing my money at everything. How could I lose? I invested in businesses, I started new businesses, I bought apartments. I lived large but it turned out I was very small and didn't know it. I had no real meaning in my life.

I had given up on the task of learning how to be a better human. I thought the game was finished and I had won.

It's only when I lost everything that my real learning began.

C) WHAT'S IMPORTANT

"Tennis is just a game, family is forever."

In every area I've studied, I've noticed something: when some people stop performing at their peak levels, they kill themselves.

I study writing a lot. At one point I realized that almost all of my favorite writers killed themselves. This scared me.

Another time I mapped the rate of suicides vs. the stock market. There was almost a perfect correlation.

I wanted to talk about this on a radio show. But they said "no."

They said, "Talking about suicide leads to suicide."

I asked, "But how do you stop suicides then?"

They never asked me back to the show.

When people associate the worth of their lives with any one activity, it's deadly.

We have to celebrate what we're good at. But also celebrate other things in life the love of another person. Our friends. Something funny. I always have to tell myself to diversify my celebrations. Celebrate the small. Not always the big.

"Meaning" is not just a victory. Meaning is a way of life.

A shortcut to meaning is to just every day ask before you go to sleep, "Who did I help today?"

D) GROWTH

"I'm feeling OK. I'm still not where I want to be at, but I'm definitely feeling better than I was."

Many studies have shown that when you compliment children on "growth" versus specific accomplishments, they perform better in the long run.

I used to think too much about my accomplishments. "What's my rank?"

Accomplishments disappear so fast. And then the people who latched onto you when you achieved those accomplishments also disappear. And you feel like a lonely failure.

Not a single person I was friends with in 1998, when I sold my first business, am I friends with now. They all left me. Or I left them. Hard to say.

Someone asked me recently where I expect to be in five years.

I never think about it. Not ever. I only try every day to improve

1% my physical, emotional, mental, and spiritual health. The results will take care of themselves.

This is the ONLY way today to plan for a successful tomorrow.

My spark maybe lit the fire. But only that 1% growth every day is the fuel to keep the fire going. Else, I burn out.

E) LOVE

"I think you have to love yourself before you fall in love. I'm still learning to love myself."

Me too.

It's a practice. Not a thing.

F) IDEA SEX

"I don't want to end my career and then start something. I like to do something while my career is still hot and I've always enjoyed designing."

Try it. Do two things at once.

Serena would have been noticed on the tennis court no matter what. But she's also known for her colorful outfits on the tennis court. Who knows? Maybe she will become one of the greatest fashion designers.

But it also underlines the importance that there is never "one thing" that we were all put on Earth to do.

We were put here to try. Nobody will grade us.

G) HATERS

"Honestly, I don't read the press. I don't know what they're saying."

Nobody escapes the HATERS. Why?

Because they hate themselves. There's no other answer.

Everyone wants to be a critic. There are critics and then there are the people who do the exact things the critics want to do.

H) PAYING THE PRICE

"There's always something you have to give up for success. Everything comes at a cost. Just what are you willing to pay for it?"

This was a quote Serena gave about whether she wanted kids.

It's brings us back to the "talent vs. skill" question. Talent lasts for five seconds. Skill requires a price. Serena now has spent 30-plus straight years practicing tennis.

Just because you pay a price doesn't mean the price was too expensive. It's what she wanted to pay. But nothing is free.

I) ACTION!

"Nothing comes to a sleeper but a dream. Our dad used to say that."

Dreams are in the head. But action creates growth, creates skill, creates excellence.

Edison didn't dream about a light bulb. He tried 10,000 experiments before one worked.

Henry Ford didn't just dream about making a car. He started three car companies and made the assembly line before he finally had success.

Steve Jobs didn't dream about the iPod. He bought one of the first Sony Walkmans and took it apart and figured out how to do it better.

Thinking keeps the adventures of life bottled in your head. Action makes you a hero.

*   *   *

I wish I could be as good at any one thing as Serena Williams is at tennis.

But I can learn from her and appreciate from a distance. I love watching her play.

She moves like a god.

If I spend my life aiming for that 1% improvement every day then I may never be the best in the world at anything. But I know I will be the best "me" at everything.

7

SEVEN UNUSUAL THINGS
I LEARNED FROM LOUIS
ARMSTRONG

I t's been more than 45 years since Louis Armstrong died. I saw a photo of him recently. He was playing the trumpet in front of the Great Sphinx while his girl watches on.

Here is a little kid whose dad abandoned him, whose mom was a prostitute, who used to play the trumpet at brothels in New Orleans and who shoveled coal in his early years, playing trumpet in front of the Sphinx.

Is this just a dream? Can life be lived so large? Have I been able to live life so large? To live to my fullest potential?

Life is truly owned by the people who dive into it and make every experience special and unique. The masters of the world don't let the oppressors—even their internal oppressors (the worst ones of all)—drag them down. Instead, they create out of thin air the experiences, the situations, the magic that constantly exist around them.

I want to be such a magician.

The photo is so beautiful, it makes me think of several things, particularly when you think about his background:

1) PAIN VS. PLEASURE

It's the moments when I've been so down and out that I thought I would never be able to raise a family, find someone to love, start or sell a business, lose a father, lose a friend, lose a marriage, etc., that I thought to myself, 'If I don't figure this out, I'm going to just die, disappear, detonate.'

And I'd figure it out. And it's one more notch that lets me LIVE.

And it's the moments when I've had the most pleasure that I've always managed to blow it, to lose my mind along with everything else.

2) TURN PAIN INTO ART

Louis Armstrong took his early pain and processed it into music. Some of those pains: father abandoned the family when he was a kid, his mother abandoned him and then became a prostitute, he lived through the Great Depression.

I can't even imagine. When I was five my mother threatened to me she would "run away." She was joking, or just having a one-day phase, but 40 years later I still viscerally feel the terror in my body at the thought of it.

Imagine actually living the terror day after day. He was totally abandoned. He worked as a little boy hauling coal to the red light district of New Orleans, where he first got his exposure to music, listening to it coming out of the brothels. And on and on.

You don't have to turn pain into music. But turn it into something. Write. Write ideas. Start a business. Get a job and blow that place away while you devise your evil plan of escape. Start today.

3) HAVE A SENSE OF SURRENDER

He was Jewish. Sort of. A Jewish family took him in and treated him like their own son, knowing he was abandoned on every side. He wore a Star of David around his neck for the rest of his life.

We hang onto whatever we can believe in that gives us some

sense of peace. It doesn't matter what it is, whether it's Buddha or Jesus or Moses or the yoga sutras. Something needs to give us a little bit of hope that there is something better out there than the spider webs gathering in the musky attic of our head.

Every day I wake up and look out the window and say to whatever it is outside of myself, "Help me save a life today."

I don't know whom I'm saying it to. It doesn't matter. Maybe there's nobody out there.

But it takes me out of my own worries and anxieties for a split second. It doesn't require faith but a tiny amount of surrender. Ask this every morning about your friends, your lovers, your employees: how can I help them just a little bit more, with the simple resources I have?

4) CONSTIPATION IS THE ROOT OF ALL EVIL

Armstrong was obsessed with laxatives and even tried to invent a few. Really, if we want to live forever, our intestines, kidneys, liver needs to be as clean as possible, however we can make that happen. Why live with shit backed up into our bodies until it touches our heart and brain?

Armstrong purged as much as possible. Keep the inside of the body clean and the music that comes out of it will be clean. He even tried to teach the Queen of England this simple concept but I'm not sure if she listened.

5) LEARN THE HISTORY OF YOUR FIELD

I always wonder why all crappy bands sound the same but the

bands that make it through history (The Beatles, U2, Led Zeppelin, Rolling Stones, etc.) have such unique sounds—regardless of whether you personally like them.

Part of it is because they studied and learned as much as possible about their chosen field. Not just how to do it, but the history of it.

I keep telling my kids, if they want to learn to sing, or to tap dance, or draw manga comics, or to do anything, learn everything you can about all the masters in your field over the past 100 years.

Learn all of their styles, learn how to mimic them, learn what influenced them. Be able to recognize them at a moment's glance. And only then will you start to develop your own unique style, which you can only then begin to master.

Louis Armstrong did this, studying every musician he could, working with every musician he could, blowing on the trumpet every day for 60 of the 70 years of his life. That's the only way to get good. To be better than the other seven billion people on the planet who would like to be as good as you would like to be. How can you compete against that? Only hard work backed by true, sincere passion.

That's how you become a magician, blowing music in front of the Sphinx.

6) BE FLEXIBLE

Armstrong moved from trumpet to trombone, storytelling, singing, and so on. He made himself useful in every circumstance where music was wanted. He wouldn't let "I can't" slow him down.

"I can't play that instrument."

"I can't sing."

He could do anything. He said "yes" to everything and then he became the best in the world at it because he knew how to become the best at something.

You can only be good at so many things. But don't limit yourself too much either. Always be looking for new opportunities to improve incrementally.

7) THERE'S ALWAYS AN OPPORTUNITY

In the Great Depression, every opportunity shut itself down. The money had run out. Some of Armstrong's compatriots went back to New Orleans to raise chickens or to just disappear into factories or famine.

Armstrong went to L.A. to play at the Cotton Club, drawing in the Hollywood crowd that was only vaguely aware that the rest of the country was in a depression.

There's always money somewhere. Every day I hear too many people complain that the world is going down. It's not. Its not worse than the Great Depression when WWII started and everybody was down and out.

And here's someone who had every aspect working against him: poor, black, broken family, lost his job, hungry, a nationwide depression, etc. And he still built an amazing career on the back of that.

Armstrong died more than 45 years ago. I barely know anything about the man. But I wish I could be one-tenth the survivor he was.

Today I'm going to try.

IF IT'S NOT HARD,
IT'S SOFT

Three were a lot of sex scenes but I didn't care. When my daughters were 13 and 16, I took them to see "Straight Outta Compton."

I'm not going to talk about the movie. Yeah, there are scenes. Yeah, they missed stuff. Whatever.

But after it finished, we kept sitting and then they had end shots of the real guys.

Ice Cube says one line: "If it's not hard, it's soft."

That is art. That is business. That is the way I need to live my life.

If a piece of writing is not hard, it's weak. It's not worth writing. It's not worth sharing.

If it's not hard, it's soft.

If you can't BLEED or KILL or SLASH YOUR GUTS with your word, then keep it to yourself.

If you can't take it to the edge, then you played it too safe. Every time.

Don't just gossip or talk to say words. Say words that are your reality, that are your pain, that express you.

If you can't change the world, then you know you have to change yourself.

Mostly, for me, if I can't say something that has really hurt me, or helped me, or changed me in some way, then I need to just shut up. I need to not write it.

Find a pain inside of you. Tease it out. This is hard. This is art.

If it's not so hot you feel like it brands you, then it's cold and you're nothing.

10

10 THINGS I LEARNED
FROM COOLIO

O K, I'm a slobbering fanboy.

I was a bit surprised when Coolio told me at the end of our interview that he thought I was obnoxious or goofy when the interview first started. But then things got real.

We came from different backgrounds completely. He was born poor and crushed. When he was 32, he had the best-selling song in the world across all genres.

When I was 32, I thought my life was over. My self-esteem was at a low. I had made so many bad decisions I thought I deserved to die. I had given up on love, on family, on my chances of success, and I thought I had gotten lucky once and never would again.

"When I was a kid I had about 50 friends I would hang out with," Coolio told me. "And now only three of them are alive and one of those three is in jail for life."

So like I said, we had completely different backgrounds on everything. And I was nervous to be talking to him.

During the prior week, I had listened to all of his albums. I had even read his cookbook. I had watched all his performances. I had watched other interviews. I didn't want to ask the same boring questions everyone else asked. I told him that.

We spoke for a little over an hour. Here's what I learned.

1) PERSEVERANCE

This is the one rule that never goes away. For all my episodes of

"The James Altucher Show," this is the ONE constant.

He told me when he was 14 years old he started writing every day. His first hit was "Fantastic Voyage" in 1994.

So he acknowledged it took him 17 years of writing every day before he had a hit.

EVERY DAY.

2) HISTORY + IDEA SEX

He described to me how he took the rap style from the '80s ("I used inflection in my voice instead of just speaking"), a song from the '70s (Stevie Wonder's "Pastime Paradise"), the gangster rap that was getting popular in the early '90s out of Compton, and combined them to create "Gangsta's Paradise."

A pyramid is built by first building a solid base. No matter what I do now, I always make sure I understand all the pieces that make up the base.

The history, the people, the styles, everything that influenced this moment right now, comes from the base of that pyramid. It's the only way to put the top piece on.

If you are an entrepreneur, a teacher, an employee trying to move up, a salesperson... you have to build that base.

3) MENTORS

Coolio took his mentors from everywhere. Real and virtual. Often the virtual mentors are even more valuable than the real ones.

"Nobody controlled the audience more than Run," he said, referring to Run from Run-D.M.C. "He controlled the floor even more than my man Mick from the Rolling Stones."

After he said that, I watched Run-D.M.C. live on YouTube. He was right. Run focused on the audience even more than the song. He'd speak directly to them and tell them what to do even if there were more than 100,000 people in the audience (Live Aid, 1985).

Then I watched Coolio perform the same song at the Billboard Music Awards (1995), the Grammys (1996), and another show (1997). I saw how he improved each time (his singing voice kept improving). I saw how he would control the audience and act, sing, rap, relate all at the same time.

4) MENTORS 2

"Ice-T was my main mentor when I started out," he told me.

I asked him what he learned from Ice-T and his answer surprised me.

"When you're being interviewed, control the interview, don't let them control you. If they ask you something you don't like, then say what you want and ignore the question."

Here's a guy who was the best in the ENTIRE WORLD at what he loved. He found real and virtual mentors everywhere.

Run was virtual. Stevie Wonder was virtual, Ice-T was real. He mentioned Rakim ("he was the first rapper to use his regular voice"). He mentioned Melle Mel ("he used a much deeper voice"). He learned everything from music to media messages from his mentors, and you can see it in the final product.

5) WORK

I asked him why people think they can just get up there and rap without putting in the 17 years. He gave me the only real answer.

"People are lazy."

And it's true. Every day I see people who have good, even great, ideas and they just want someone to write them a check so they can quit their jobs and start their company and then sell their company.

You know how many times that happens in life?

Basically zero. Even Mark Zuckerberg had 500,000 users when he got his first check from Peter Thiel.

Coolio saw what was happening to all the people around him. He would read, he would write, he would work on his rapping, every day, so the same thing didn't happen to him.

6) MONEY

Two things about money.

First, he mentioned that "if you do anything for the money or the girls, then stop. There's plenty of ways you can do something easier. If you want to be the best, you have to do it for love."

This coming from the man who rapped, "I'm an educated fool with money on my mind."

Second, he mentioned to me that the value of the dollar had been going down 4% per year since 2009.

"How do you even know that?" I said. I didn't know it and I supposedly follow stuff like that. He said, "I have to make sure I protect my money. I have kids, family."

7) TRANSFORM HATE INTO LOVE

I asked him about cooking. I have it right in front of me, his cookbook, "Cooking with Coolio," as I write this. I watched his shows on YouTube. He's serious about cooking.

"When I was a kid, we had a certain way of eating because we never knew when we were going to get food. My daughter saw me once and told me, 'Stop eating like that.' I realized I hated eating, so that's why I ate like that. I rushed it down.

"So I started to cook. I wanted to cook like my mom. To learn to love to cook like when I used to love my mom's cooking."

"How long have you been cooking?" I asked him.

"12 years."

So again, he wanted to get good at something. He wanted to take something he hated and turn it into something he loved and even turn it into a career option. Twelve years of work.

8) REALITY

"It's sad to me that a song I wrote almost 20 years ago is the main song people want to hear when I tour," he said.

"Every stop I make, I have to play that song."

I think it's OK to peak in one area. But learning to be the best in the world at something is a skill.

It's almost like there's a grammar of success. When you learn to use that grammar to learn one language, you can also apply the same techniques to learn to be a success in new areas.

The key is to not keep pushing in one area of life, but to use that meta-grammar of success to keep changing and learning and becoming a success in other areas.

It's the one common thing I see with everyone I interview. Mark Cuban, Tim Ferriss, Arianna Huffington, etc.

9) I RELAXED

I was really nervous at first. Would I totally screw this one up like I did the interview with Biz Markie?

Someone on Twitter even said, "Here's what your interview with Coolio will go like… 'So "Gangsta's Paradise" was your big hit,' you'll say and he'll say, 'Na na na, I had a lot of other hits,' and then there will be 45 minutes of tense conversation."

Which is funny because that's exactly what I was afraid was going to happen.

But instead, during the interview I just relaxed.

I asked the questions I wanted to ask and when he gave an answer I was curious about, I would just ask, "Why is that?" I was talking to him like we were friends.

He was a friendly guy and even though there was probably zero in common at any single point in our lives, I made sure I was going to have a fun time in the conversation.

It took me a few minutes to relax, which is maybe why he thought I sounded obnoxious or goofy at the beginning of the interview.

But during the interview with Coolio, I leaned back against the wall and just listened and blurted out questions whenever I was curious and wanted to learn more rather than force it.

10) HIS FEEDBACK

"But then the interview changed," he told me at the end, "and you got me to reveal some deep shit. Some shit I didn't want to get into. Kudos on your skills," he said.

And that made me feel good.

I've interviewed probably close to 3,000 people in the past 20 years in all sorts of situations, but that was the best compliment I've ever gotten.

Then he said, "James, if you could see what I am seeing now, you would want to switch places with me."

"What are you seeing?"

And he told me. Although that part I have to keep to myself.

THE SECRET
of
ALL ART

Steven Wright, the comedian, helps Louis C.K. write his TV shows. He's the ONLY person Louis C.K. trusts to help him.

Here's a Steven Wright joke. Picture him saying it in a very droll monotone way:

"It's a small world, but I wouldn't want to have to paint it."

Yesterday I read that Steven Wright has read everything Kurt Vonnegut has ever written.

Yay!

I think I've also read everything Kurt Vonnegut has ever written.

So once again I am indirectly connected to Louis C.K. We're like blood brothers.

Kurt Vonnegut has written almost 20 bestselling books. His book *Cat's Cradle* is required reading in almost every high school. I love him.

But... he was a total failure.

By 1968, after 20 years of writing, all of his books were out of print. He was broke. Nobody had ever heard of him. Nobody cared. His career was over.

Some of those books later became massive bestsellers: *Cat's Cradle, The Sirens of Titan, Mother Night,* and so on.

I was talking to Casey Neistat, who has over a BILLION You-

Tube views. He wanted to be a filmmaker. Would he have made it in Hollywood?

He said, "My first films were garbage. I've been doing this for 15 years."

He said, "I make sure every one-twenty-fourth of a second in every video moves the story forward."

Casey isn't stopped by gatekeepers. He makes a video every day and uploads it. And every day, 500,000 people watch his videos.

"I don't care what other people think," he said. "Original artists don't care."

I unfortunately care. I care too much. I hide under my pillows caring. I know I shouldn't care.

Sometimes I feel like a little child around all of these people I admire.

When I left Casey's studio, I dropped all my equipment. I forgot my phone. He had to run after me. I care so much I get nervous.

Kurt Vonnegut had gatekeepers. He was dependent on publishers and bookstores.

Finally he published a book that was acceptable to both ("Slaughterhouse Five") and all of his books started coming back in print and bit by bit, he became one of the bestselling authors ever.

Here's what I think all great artists do:

1) *They have a deeply personal emotional anchor they can tie their work to.*

For Kurt Vonnegut, he was dramatically affected by the fire-bombing of Dresden, Germany, where he was a prisoner of war.

About 130,000 people died in a single day. Compared with 90,000 in Hiroshima. Kurt Vonnegut survived and his job after that was to dig up all the bodies.

When he anchors a book (in *Slaughterhouse Five*, for instance, he anchors to the most horrific moment of his life), he can go crazy after that: time travel, other planets, placing the author as a side character in the book, all sorts of experimentation.

It doesn't matter because he can always pull back to the emotional anchor when he needs to. And then we all relate.

No emotional anchor = no art. No meaning.

Another example: The Harry Potter series.

The emotional anchor: an orphan, mistreated by relatives, wants to feel special.

The craziness: Off to wizard's school to fight bad magic everywhere!

Another example: "Carrie."

Anchor: Socially outcast girl with overly religious and strict mother.

Craziness: Rains blood on everyone at the prom.

None of these writers use fancy language. They get their emotional anchor. Then they go crazy. They are not "trained" writers. They write.

I get scared sometimes. I feel my emotional anchor is how I lost my money in 2001-2002 and then made it back. Blah, blah, blah, I was suicidal. Blah, blah, write 10 ideas a day. Be grateful.

Alright already!

There are only so many times I can write about that. Too many times and it becomes boring.

Every single day, art and innovation are right outside the emotional prison of your comfort zone.

When Vonnegut left out his emotional anchor, I think his writing started to decline.

He tried to cater to an audience instead of focusing on what was right outside his comfort zone and continuing to explore.

What are your emotional anchors? The events that staple the timeline of your life to something that totally destroyed who you thought you were?

They can be small moments or big moments.

These are the moments where you choose yourself.

Vonnegut's critical tips on writing are a must-read for anybody who wants to create or innovate or explore.

I hope when I grow up I can one day be as good as Casey, or Vonnegut, or Steven Wright. (Or, shhh, Louis C.K.)

*   *   *

Actually, one more piece of writing advice from Louis CK.

I heard this in an interview Tim Ferriss did with BJ Novak.

Louis CK says, "If you think about something three times in a week, you have to write it."

That could be a good shortcut for finding out what your emotional anchor is (this week).

5

5 UNUSUAL THINGS I LEARNED FROM ISAAC ASIMOV

T he second time the police were called to pick me up, I was 15 years old. I was originally going to type "the first time" but then I realized that I had gotten in serious trouble one time before. But that's another story. First I have to confess to my kids about it.

But back to this second time. I was with Robert Levinson and we had just gone to see Isaac Asimov speak. We were both fans of Asimov. I loved his Foundation series. It's about the decline of the Galactic Empire. A group of people use statistics ("psychohistory") to determine that the decline will last 30,000 years, so they need to store up as much intelligence as possible before the end comes. The series was three books and written in the early 1950s and is still a great series. I reread it in 2003 but more on that in a second. His other major series, that I was not really interested in, resulted in the movie: "I, Robot" starring Will Smith.

I can't remember what Asimov spoke about. It was the first time I was in the room with such a personality and I think I was overwhelmed by it.

Afterward, Rob and I went to Rob's house. He had just gotten a moped. I had never ridden one so we were riding around on it when the police stopped us and asked if I was James Altucher. If the same thing happened to me now, I know my auto-reflex answer would be, "No, but I think I saw him going in the other direction."

In any case, my grandparents had called the police when I didn't report in instantly after the Asimov talk. They were worried I had gone and joined some Asimovian cult, as if there were one. They couldn't stop talking about it all night. I only wanted to ride a moped for once in my life.

I wasn't even that into science fiction other than that Foundation series and a few stories. I was more into the fantasy genre. Tolkien and Zelazny were my heroes. Not Asimov.

But I recently read his memoir and some of his shorter works and it brought back memories and how much I really learned from him:

A) PROLIFICNESS

Asimov wrote 467 published books. Some of them were anthologies. But even on those he wrote in-depth intros and intros to each story. Most of his books were non-fiction, which I think he viewed as easier to write than novels. He estimated that after the invention of the word processor, he published 1,700 words a day on average. Most people have a hard time writing even 500 words a day, let alone 1,700 words a day.

So I've decided. I want to write 100 books. As long as I have something to offer I'm going to try to write at least 1,000 words worth publishing each day. A lot of great authors sacrifice quantity for perceived quality. Like Thomas Pynchon's meager portfolio of books, or J.D. Salinger's. But Asimov shows you can do both (and I would take the Foundation series over Pynchon's "Gravity's Rainbow" any day).

B) A SENSE OF WONDER

In his memoir, he writes that his favorite short story that he wrote was "The Last Question." I couldn't remember whether I had ever read it. I went to the bookstore at the Grand Central train station in N.Y.C. and picked up a collection of his stories.

On the train ride, I noticed "The Last Question" was in it so I started reading. Within a few lines I remembered I had read it at least 30 years earlier. And I even remembered what the last line of the story was going to be.

And it was true. It was his best story. It was one of my favorite stories ever and I had constantly recalled it over the past 30 years even though I had long forgotten the title. It was beautiful, and re-reading it again brought back that initial sense of wonder I felt 30 years ago.

I felt like a 13-year-old again. It washed off all the sense of dirty responsibility I have now—kids, bills, colleagues, investors, to myself and the goals I've set for myself now that the hopes of youth are tinged with regret, and the regrets I'll feel in the future that are my meager hopes now. What goals? What hopes? They all disappeared for a split second into that last line and into the question that spit it out.

C) A GROUP TO GROW UP WITH

In the 1940s, my three favorite science fiction writers Isaac Asimov, Arthur C. Clarke, and Robert Heinlein (probably my favorite of the three), were "the big three" of science fiction. They were the three best then and probably the three best ever.

And they were all friends who challenged each other, competed, saw each other whenever possible, and built up a companionship with each other that lasted for decades.

It reminds me of how Burroughs, Kerouac, and Ginsberg formed a literary bond that became the Beat Generation of writing. In almost any science, art, culture, literature, you can find these groups.

We won't know now, or for decades even, but I wonder if the same thing will happen in the relatively new genre of "blog-ature." Doing more with a blog than "10 tips to get more blog users" or "Here's what happened today to my 5-year-old."

A good quality blog post has particular qualities that make it different from any other literary genre:

* **IT HAS TO CAPTURE YOU** from the first sentence. Short stories written in the New Yorker don't, for instance. The New Yorker has a captive audience: someone bought the magazine and they are going to sit and read that story no matter how bored they are. When someone reads a blog they probably already have ten tabs open on their browser. They can flip away in a microsecond if you don't grab them and hold them.

* **YOU HAVE TO TELL A STORY.** A simple list is no good. Nobody is going to believe "10 ways to make a million dollars" if you don't tell your personal and painful story about how you made it.

* **YOU HAVE TO SOLVE A PROBLEM.** People historically use computers to solve problems. They don't read fiction on computers, for instance. A blog, even if it's a blog told in mostly story format, has to provide a solution to some personal problem or world problem.

* **HONESTY.** Blogs from day one are personal and honest. The best ones bleed all over the screen. A good story has an underdog. A good blog has someone that the predators have targeted. Does the blogger come out alive? Does the reader find catharsis with the bloggers rescue?

When I write "10 reasons to quit your job," it's not because I want you to quit your job. It's because I've had jobs and they have made me sick: the backstabbing, the subservience, the insignificance of being one cog in a meaningless machine that grinds away to produce... what? More Americana? Who did I help? Who are you helping?

D) HUMBLE VANITY

Asimov has a quote in his memoir and I can't find it at the moment but he basically says, "I'm the most brilliant man there is. And this is not being vain. It would only be vanity if you can find someone more intelligent than me!"

And he's only half-joking but then throughout the book we see that he is horrible at chess, not the most smooth with women, not the best husband or father, and on and on he admits to all his foibles while still grasping onto his one trophy, that he's is basically the best at whatever he wants to be the best at.

And why not think that way? Why suffer from a false humility that we all know is the worst kind of vanity. His vanity is honest and earned. But he is also half-joking because he doesn't care what we think. But he does care! It's only a half-joke. Which makes it even funnier. Or not. I don't even know what I'm saying anymore. But you get it. I got it.

E) TRADING

Yes, Isaac Asimov saved my financial life. I was losing everything I ever worked for. I needed to make some money. I had a lot of time on my hands because I had no job. The dot-com boom had busted. Nobody would even talk to me or have anything to do with me. I had been a quick solar flare in the supernova of dot-com finance and now I had been absorbed back into the black hole at the center.

So I re-read the Foundation series by Asimov. The premise is that with the use of statistics (he called it "psychohistory") you can gather up all the prior history and use it to predict the future.

So that's exactly what I did. I loaded up all the historical data of the stock market into some software and wrote programs to figure out what would happen next.

So, for instance, what happened the prior 90 times that MSFT opened up 5% down? Oh, if you buy at the open, then 89 out of 90 times it went up 2% before 10 a.m. OK, I'm a buyer. And that's how I would do all my trades and made money almost every day trading for the next three years.

During this time I went to Las Vegas to visit with Jack Binion, the owner of Binion's Gambling Hall and Hotel and a bunch of riverboat casinos on the Mississippi. I stayed at his house and it was the first and only time I was ever in Las Vegas without staying at a hotel. He was in the process of selling all his casinos for a cool $3 or $4 billion. I wanted him to invest some money with me.

I remember three things about that visit, other than that Binion ultimately did not invest with me:

1. It was so hot in May in Las Vegas that we had to basically wake up at 4 or 5 a.m. to get some outside pool time. Then a little later in the day we drove out into the desert, which I had never done before.

2. Jack said, "OK, let's go eat at my favorite restaurant."

Jack Binion was a billionaire, everyone in Las Vegas knew him, and we were going to go to his favorite restaurant.

I assumed gourmet food, expensive wine, and high-priced hookers hanging all over us at whatever top secret restaurant in the best casino was going to host us that evening.

We got in the car and head straight for... Cheesecake Factory.

And then he gave his name and we waited in line for 45 MINUTES.

Nice, humble guy. And the food was amazing.

3. I started to describe what I did. How I made my trades. His nephew piped up, "It sounds like a book I'm reading, 'Foundation' by Isaac Asimov."

"You're right!"

But, billionaires stay billionaires by not handing out their money to any kid who comes in with a science fiction book strategy for trading the markets.

Asimov's dead now. Unfortunately he died of AIDS from a blood transfusion. And my grandparents are dead. So they can't call the police on me anymore (twice was enough).

Jack Binion sold all his casinos and made billions. Rob Levinson graduated from mopeds to now doing highly specialized mechanic work on fancy race cars. I don't day trade anymore.

But I still want that sense of wonder that hit me for only a few moments in my childhood. I want it back. I want to know the answer to the Last Question over and over again, forever. I want it now. I don't want it to ever leave me again.

ARE YOU THERE,
JUDY BLUME? IT'S
ME, JAMES

J udy Blume saved my life.

When I was 10, I read all of her young adult books (82 million books sold), "Tales of a Fourth Grade Nothing," "Blubber," etc.

Then I memorized the sex scene in "Forever..." Then I memorized ALL the sex scenes in "Wifey."

She wrote a book, *Are You There God? It's Me, Margaret,* about a somewhat lonely girl who talks with God to figure out all the changes puberty and childhood brings to all of us.

And then for my podcast, I SPOKE TO JUDY BLUME (BAM! Massive name drop).

It's so blah to say "10 things I learned from..." when it comes to her. I learned how to be a human being.

But when I spoke to her, I was surprised at her humility and the wisdom that kept pouring out. She has a very sweet voice and she laughs a lot.

And I thought, "I still love her." She's 77. I'd definitely marry her. I'd have babies with her.

So... three things I learned while talking to her that I think everyone can benefit from. Artists and entrepreneurs and friends.

The reason why she can sell 82 million books is she knows the most important things in life and just says them.

A) NORMAL WILL KILL YOU

She got married at 19. Had two kids. And was constantly sick.

"When I was a kid, I constantly had all of these stories in my head," she said, "but then I got trapped on this 'normal' path—the marriage, the suburbs, the kids, and I let the stories stop.

"So I started getting sick all the time. These weird illnesses that the doctors couldn't figure out.

"I started writing. The stories just started to flow. All of my books. And I didn't get sick again."

Nothing wrong with suburbs and kids.

But every day, I feel she is telling me, you have to unlock your creativity.

If you don't let it flow, it will be trapped inside, it will mutate, it will kill you.

Every day, create.

B) FRIENDSHIP

People discover their lives through the words of their friends. Everyone needs someone to turn to. To touch in some way.

We learn about our bodies, about morality, about better ways to live life, not from the supernatural but from the natural—from our friends.

In her books, as young kids figure out their insecurities, their sexualities, their fears of change, they turn to their friends.

"The most important thing in life," she told me, "more important than anything else by far, is friendship."

It was almost like she was telling me my own story right now.

I'm so grateful for the friendships I have right this second. Without them, I'm afraid I would be dead.

Every day I try to build those up and improve them. To water them and nourish them and love them. It's a matter of life and death.

Today I'm going to do something for the people who love me and who I love.

And tomorrow. And the next day.

C) BE THE ONE PEOPLE TURN TO

She didn't know what her novels would be about. What their themes would be.

"I just wrote."

But when she was done, she was the one that 80 million kids turned to.

It's not because she solved my problems. Or my friends' problems. Or anything.

It's because she showed how she solved her confusions. She gave us permission to be afraid. To be confused. To want to understand our bodies and our relationships and our friends and loves and what was right and wrong and beautiful and fun in it all.

People often say a lie: "Solve other people's problems and you will be successful."

This is never true. Never. Show us how you solved your problems. Even if you never solved them, still show how you tried. You can give us permission to be confused just like you were.

How do you show us? Write something. Create something. Build something. Talk to people. It doesn't matter.

Don't stand on a pedestal.

Come under the sheets with me, where I have a flashlight and I'm reading what you have to say long after I should've gone to sleep.

Don't lecture me. Show me.

Don't give me rules. Give me permission.

Don't be aloof and far away. Be my friend.

Judy Blume was there for me when I was a kid. And she was there for me on my podcast in ways she probably doesn't even realize.

After 40 years of reading you, I don't think this tiny "thank you" is enough. Now that I've talked to you I feel like I can just drop the mic. BOOM!

Thank you.

SIX THINGS I LEARNED
from
CHARLES BUKOWSKI

Charles Bukowski was disgusting, his fiction is awful, he's been called a misogynist, overly simplistic, the worst narcissist (probably all of the above are true to an extent), and whenever there's a collection of "greatest American writers" he's never included.

And yet... he's probably the greatest American writer ever. Whether you've read him or not, and most have not, there are six things worthy of learning from an artist like Bukowski.

I consider *Ham on Rye* by Bukowski probably the greatest American novel ever written. It's an autobiographical novel (as are all his novels except *Pulp,* which is so awful it's unreadable) about his childhood, being beaten by his parents, avoiding war, and beginning his life of destitution, hardship, alcoholism, and the beginnings of his education as a writer.

I'm almost embarrassed to admit he's an influence. Many people hate him and I'm much more afraid of being judged than he ever was.

1) HONESTY

His first four novels are autobiographical. He details the suffering he had as a child (putting his parents in a very bad light, but he didn't care), his experiences with prostitutes, his lack of interest in holding down a job, his horrible experiences and lack of real respect for the women he was in relationships with, and on and on.

His fiction and poetry document thoroughly the people he hates, the authors he despises, the establishment he couldn't care less about. (By the way, he hated the anti-establishment just as much.

One quote about a potential plan from the hippie movement: "Run a pig for president? What the fuck is that? It excited them. It bored me."

Most fiction writers do what fiction writers do: they make stuff up. They tell stories that come from their imagination. Bukowski wasn't really able to do that. Whenever he attempted fiction (his last novel being a great example), it fell flat. Even his poetry is non-fiction.

There's one story he wrote (I forget the name) where he's sitting in a bar and he wants to be alone and some random guy starts talking to him.

"It's horrible about all those girls who were burned," the guy said.

And Bukowski says (I'm writing this from memory, so the words may be off), "I don't know."

And the guy and everyone else in the bar start yelling, "This guy doesn't care that all those little girls burned to death."

But Bukowski was honest: "It was a newspaper headline. If it happened in front of me, I'd probably feel different about it." And he refused to back down and stayed in the bar until closing time.

He had very few boundaries for how far his honesty could go. He never wrote about his daughter after she reached a certain age. That's about the only boundary I can find.

Every other writer has so many things they can't write about: family, spouses, exes, children, jobs, bosses, colleagues, friends.

That's why they make stuff up.

Bukowski didn't let himself get hampered by that, so we see real, raw honesty, a real anthropological survey of being down and out for 60-plus years without anything being held back. No other writer before or since has done that.

For a particular example, see his novel "Women," which details every sexual nuance of every woman who dared to sleep with him after he achieved some success. Most of these women were horrified after the book came out.

I try as hard as possible to remove all boundaries.

2) PERSISTENCE

Bukowski got two stories published when he was young (24 and 26 years old) but almost all of his stories were rejected by publishers.

So he quit writing for 10 years.

Then, in the mid-1950s, he started up again. He submitted tons of poems and stories everywhere he could. It took him years to get published. It took him even more years to get really noticed.

And it took him about 15 years of writing every day, writing thousands of poems and stories before he finally started making a living as a writer. He wrote his first novel at the age of 49 and it was financially successful. After 25 years of plugging away at it he was finally a successful writer.

25 years!

ople give up much earlier, much younger. Both my grand-
d father wanted to be musicians, for instance. Both gave
up in their 20s and 30s and took what they thought was the safer
route (the safer route being, in my opinion, what ultimately killed
both of them).

And this persistence was while he was going through three mar-
riages, dozens of jobs, and non-stop alcoholism. Some of this is
documented (poorly) in the movie "Barfly" but I think a better
movie about Bukowski is the indie film "Factotum," based on the
book, which details the 10 years he was going from job to job,
woman to woman, just trying to survive as an alcoholic in a world
that kept beating him down.

He wrote his first novel in 19 days. Michael Hemmingson, who
I write about below, wrote me and said Bukowski had to finish
that novel so fast because he was desperately afraid he was going
to be a failure at being a successful writer and didn't want to disappoint John Martin, who had essentially given him an advance
for the novel.

3) SURVIVAL

When I think "constant alcoholic," I usually equate that with being a homeless bum. Bukowski, at some deep level, realized that
he needed to survive. He couldn't just be a homeless bum and kill
himself, no matter how many disappointments he had.

He worked countless factory jobs (the basis of the non-fiction
novel, "Factotum") but even that wasn't stable enough for him.
Finally, he took a job for the U.S. Government (you can't get
more stable) working in the post office for 11 years.

He didn't miss child support payments (although he constantly wrote about how ugly the mother of his child was), and as far as I know he was never homeless or totally down and out from his early 30s until the time he started having success as a writer.

And despite writing about the overwhelming poverty he had, he did have a small inheritance from his father, a savings account he built up, and a steady paycheck. The post office job is documented, in full, in his first "novel" called, appropriately, "Post Office." (Many people think that's his best novel but I put it third or fourth behind "Ham on Rye" and "Factotum" and possibly "Women.")

He also wrote a novel, "Hollywood," about the blow-by-blow experience of doing the movie "Barfly." All the names are changed (hence its claim to be fiction) but once you figure out who everyone is, it's totally non-fiction. Like all of his other novels (not counting "Pulp," which was the worst American novel ever written and published).

4) DISCIPLINE

Imagine working a brutal 10-hour shift at the post office, coming home and arguing with your wife or girlfriend, or half-girlfriend/half-prostitute who was living with you, finishing off three or four six-packs of beer and then… writing.

He did it every day. Most people want to write that novel, or finish that painting, or start that business, but have zero discipline to actually sit down and do it. If there was a talent Bukowski had that I can't figure out how he got, it's that discipline.

When he was younger (early 20s, late teens) he spent almost ev-

: library, falling in love with all the great writers. The
.ve been so great it superseded almost everything else

He ɥau ͟. write like them or he really felt like he would die. He
had to "put down a good line" as he would say. And every day he
would try. And good, bad, or ugly, he probably ultimately ended
up publishing (many posthumously) everything he ever wrote.

I try to match that discipline. Even when I don't post a blog post,
I write seven days a week, every morning. At least 1,000 words
and a completed post. I used to do this in my 20s when I was
trying to write fiction. My minimum then was 3,000 words. I did
that for five years.

It adds up. The average book is 60,000 words. If you can
write 1,000 words a day then you'll have six books by the end
of the year.

5) HIS "LITERARY MAP"

Bukowski was inspired by several writers and he inspired many
more. Some of my favorite writers come from both categories.
He was probably most inspired by three writers: Louis-Ferdinand
Céline, Knut Hamsun, and John Fante.

I highly recommend Céline's "Journey to the End of the Night."
Celine is almost a more raw version of Bukowski. He was constantly angry and trying to survive and doing whatever it took to
survive.

The thing about Bukowski, as opposed to many other writers, is
he didn't concern himself with flowery images or beautiful sun-
sets. He totally wrote as if he were speaking to you. Céline does

that to an extreme, but he's so raw and smart that the way he "speaks" is like an insane person trying to spew out as much venom as possible. His first book is a masterpiece and I often read it in my pre-writing hour every morning for inspiration.

John Fante wrote the underappreciated "Ask the Dust," which was completely forgotten until Bukowski's publisher republished it, as well as all of Fante's other books. (I also recommend the movie with Colin Farrell and a naked Salma Hayek.)

Bukowski was almost afraid to admit how much Fante directly influenced him. He wrote in one short story:

> *"I realized that admitting John Bante had been such a great influence on my writing might detract from my own work, as if part of me was a carbon copy, but I didn't give a damn. It's when you hide things that you choke on them."*

(Note he spelled "Fante" as "Bante." That's the extent of Bukowski's fiction.)

Another interesting thing is the last line. Nothing flowery, nothing descriptively beautiful. Yet a line like that is what made Bukowski unique and one of the best writers ever, getting at the hidden truth of what was really happening in his head, rather than telling yet another boring story filled with flowery descriptions like most books and stories try to do.

Then there are the authors Bukowski influenced. Michael Hemmingson wrote an excellent review of Bukowski in the book "The Dirty Realism Duo: Bukowski and Carver," which I highly recommend. Raymond Carver comes from the same genre of down-

and-out, realist, simple writing that was mostly autobiographical (although that's a little less clear in Carver's case).

I'd also throw Denis Johnson's book of short stories, "Jesus' Son," in that category (Johnson studied with Carver) and more recently, books like Hemmingson's "Crack Hotel," "The Comfort of Women," "My Dream Date (Rape) with Kathy Acker," and other stories. I'm dying to find other writers in this category.

I read how Denis Johnson needed $10,000 to pay the IRS. So he threw together some vignettes he had forgotten about, called the collection "Jesus' Son," sent it off to Jonathan Galassi and said, "Here, you can have these if you pay the IRS." So I added Galassi as a Facebook friend and asked him if he could tell me one author in Denis Johnson's league, but I'm still waiting for a response.

I wish I could find more writers like these. Perhaps William Vollmann, who wrote "Butterfly Stories," but his bigger fiction is too difficult for me to read. (Anecdote: he wrote the afterward to the recently re-published Céline's "Journey to the End of the Night," so all of these writers tend to recognize their common lineage.)

6) POETRY

I really hate poetry. When I open up The New Yorker (blech!) and read the latest poems in there, I can't understand them. They all seem like gibberish to me. They all seem too intellectual.

And yet, out of all the poets I've read, the only ones I really like are Bukowski, Raymond Carver, and Denis Johnson. Poetry al- them to master the art of making each and every word e and powerful.

It was this training that allowed them to destroy the competition when they sat down to write their longer pieces. It makes me want to try my hand at poetry but even the word "poetry" sounds so pseudo-intellectual I just have no interest in doing it.

Bukowski: Alcoholic, postal worker, misogynist (there's a video you can easily find on YouTube where he must be almost 60 and he literally kicks his wife in anger while he's being interviewed), anti-war, anti-peace, anti-everything, hated everyone, probably insecure, extremely honest, and had to write every day or it would kill him.

In his own words, words I hope to live by: "What a joy it must be to be a truly great writer, even if it means a shotgun at the finish."

WHAT I LEARNED ABOUT LEADERSHIP FROM A NOTORIOUS DRUG DEALER

" We want you to come out here and interview Freeway Rick Ross on stage."

"Who?"

I was talking to Jayson Gaignard. I don't really know anything about anything so Jayson had to explain, and then I looked up Rick. And then I got obsessed.

Rick Ross had sold about $1 billion worth of crack cocaine during his "career."

I read every book. I read his autobiography. I read about a dozen articles. I watched three documentaries.

I flew out to Jayson's MastermindTalks in Napa Valley.

Seth Godin has great advice about speaking at conferences: If you speak at a conference, either do it for free because you love it, or charge FULL RETAIL.

I flew out to Jayson's conference for free.

I was really nervous because I knew I had nothing at all in common with Rick.

Maybe he would hate me. Some nerdy Jewish guy who thinks he knows everything.

I had written down about 100 questions but I knew I wouldn't look at my notes during the interview. I then rewrote them from memory. And then rewrote them again.

I knew the questions I rewrote the most were the ones that were probably most interesting to me.

There were many things I didn't care much about: politics, legal issues, the Iran-Contra Affairs (Rick was fooled by the CIA into providing drug profits to the Contras).

The rise of gang violence was an issue, so before the interview I had lunch with Rick and asked about that.

He told me that while he was there, everyone working for one cause: making money, and they knew that if homicide police came in then that would be the end of the money.

"There was less gang violence when I was in charge," he said, "because we were all getting rich."

Rick Ross's most active years were from 1981-1988. Basically $1 billion worth of crack went through his organization. His connection was from Nicaragua. His distribution was all the gangs that he grew up with in South Central L.A.

His family broke up when he was 4. He grew up amid non-stop violence. He watched his uncle kill his aunt. Gang violence was an everyday occurrence.

He didn't learn to read or write, so when he was 18 he was kicked out of high school and kicked off the tennis team where he was an aspiring champion. That was his one chance, he felt, to get out of the ghetto.

He was on the street and needed to make money without an education, a family, and the ability to read or write.

He asked an old high school teacher for advice on how he could make money. The teacher suggested he sell drugs.

So he sold drugs. And instead of spending his profits, Rick kept doubling and doubling until all the other dealers were now buying from him and Rick was using his scale to drive his own costs down.

Eventually he was the main connection in all of the United States, buying up to $5 million worth of cocaine A DAY.

He had spent, over various periods, close to 20 years in jail. Now his main goal was to lecture kids in jail and school on how to avoid the situation he had been in.

Here's what I gather were his main rules on leadership. How to lead a billion-dollar organization where many of the people below him ("all of them," Rick said and the crowd laughed) carried guns.

A) TRY TO GET THE PEOPLE WORKING FOR YOU TO BE MORE SUCCESSFUL THAN YOU

"I wanted the same for them and for them to even surpass me."

They might not always take it. But give them the chance to be as successful as you and they will take that example to the people below them.

B) HONESTY

This sounds strange coming from a drug kingpin but there aren't any lawyers or courts to track down liars. Honesty is the law in that game.

When there are lawyers, people lie and deceive and betray. When everything is based on your word and everyone is carrying guns, honesty is the rule.

"If there was any funny business, I'd rather not deal with them anymore, or be very careful with them in the future."

C) BE VERY LOW KEY

Nobody ever saw Rick being flashy. He was so low key that even when he was running almost $500 million a year, the police had no idea what he looked like.

Part of this was a decentralized structure. People several layers below him in the organization would not have any contact with him and would have to deal with conflicts at their level.

"I had to show by example how to manage, so the people underneath me would know what to do instead of me being always involved."

D) ONLY DO THE ESSENTIAL

Rick arranged the top level contacts between his sellers and his buyers. Then he stepped back.

Everything else had to be dealt with by the people who worked for him and the people who worked for them.

"Everyone knew what they had to do."

And if they didn't, they stopped being part of the food chain.

E) DON'T MAKE IT ABOUT THE MONEY

Again, odd advice from a mega drug lord.

Rick poured many of his profits back into his neighborhood.

This was in part to give back, to contribute. But at the same time, it was strategic.

When he went to jail at one point and his bail was set at over $1 million, the million had to come from legitimate enterprises. So Rick could not supply his own bail.

Instead, every family on the block he grew up on put up their own homes as bail in order to get Rick out of jail.

When you make it about something other than the money, the benefits never stop, since money is only a tiny byproduct of the reasons we live, we do things, we strive for success.

F) REDUCE CONFRONTATIONS

When things have the possibility of getting incredibly violent, reduce confrontation as quickly as possible.

Often Rick would simply pay off or write off any losses on people who were no longer fitting in with the organization, rather than have a confrontation with them.

Violence could bring in a whole new set of problems. Better to take a loss and move on and now worry about it.

G) FREEMIUM

It's almost a cliché, but Rick told how he went to Cincinnati, stayed with a friend and told him to invite 10 of his friends over.

Then when everyone was there, he gave everyone a free sample and told them if they were interested to come back in a week and buy the next batch.

Everyone came back. Sometimes the sooner you charge in a business, the quicker you put a ceiling on your potential for expansion. This is true whether your business is drugs or Facebook.

H) ASSUME THE WORST

"I always knew I was going to go to jail," Rick said.

But he wasn't going to sit around and wait for it to happen. He owned over a dozen houses so nobody knew where he was.

He barricaded the houses with multiple iron fences so that it would take the police over an hour to smash their way in, and by then everyone would be gone.

He would leave town for months at a time. He would put extra profits into "legitimate" businesses like a car parts company and hotels.

He always assumed the worst, so that's how he was able to diversify all the potential ways he could succeed.

* * *

At the end of the interview Rick described how he lear
read and write in prison.

He said that the U.S. jail system spends $45,000 a yea
oner but refuses to buy prisoners books.

These are the books he recommended:

* *As a Man Thinketh* by James Allen
* *Awaken the Giant Within* by Tony Robbins
* *Think and Grow Rich* by Napoleon Hill
* *The Richest Man in Babylon* by George Samuel Clason

He said that when he was broke and his mother was broke and his
community was broke and he couldn't read or write and had no
education or prospects, this seemed like the only way out.

When asked what he could've have done differently, he para-
phrased "The Richest Man in Babylon."

"When I was young I asked the most successful person I knew
how I could make some money," he said.

He looked down for a few seconds. Looked back up at the audience. Paused.

"I asked the wrong person."

DAYMOND JOHN SCHOOLS ME ON "THE POWER OF BROKE"

I was starving all the time. I lived in one room, had one futon and had a three-inch screen on the floor next to the futon. But the TV didn't work because you needed cable and I couldn't afford that.

So I started a business. Many people think 'I have an idea' and then they want to raise $10 million or something outrageous.

I didn't have any ideas. But I was good at this new thing, the Internet, and I convinced people they needed to build websites.

Was I right or wrong? Does a company need a website?

Who knew back then? Nobody knew.

But I was broke and hungry and wanted money to purchase some small piece of freedom so I could do what I loved—write.

So I sold the few skills I had to masters who would pay me, and I got to work.

Which is why I was excited to read the book "The Power of Broke" by Daymond John, founder of FUBU and, $6 billion in sales later, a star of the ABC show "Shark Tank."

Daymond came on my podcast. He told me first about a time when he was no longer broke and why NOT being broke got him in trouble.

"I started a record label," he said. "We made the fanciest videos, the best ads, we got the best artists, we made an album.

"We spent $3 million on ads and videos and we sold $1 million worth of records.

"This reminded me about how I should always get back to that feeling of being broke. That feeling of taking care of risk, of struggling to maximize every strength. That feeling of hustle that puts you back on the street."

He got the entrepreneurial bug when his mom taught him how to sew wool caps and he sewed 80 of them out of fabric he bought for almost nothing, sold them for $10 each and made $800.

"Did you go back the next day and sew more?" I asked him.

"No," he said and he paused. "I went back THE NEXT HOUR and sewed more."

Within a few years, his FUBU line had $350 million in sales. Within a decade or so he had sold $6 billion worth of clothes.

In his book, he tells story after story of people who went from broke to wealth.

"People always say you need money to make money," he said to me. "This is wrong. If it were true why would half the Forbes 500 of the richest people in the world start with nothing?

"In fact if I had ZERO money when I started that record label, it probably would've worked. Instead, I went in there with the wrong mindset and I failed. I wasn't hungry enough."

We talked for an hour. He told me lots of stories from the book.

I was trying to write down notes of what he said so could I learn. No matter how many businesses I've started and failed at (with a success here or there) I always want to learn more.

This is what he said:

• COMMUNITY

Find your community or your following. He talked about a teen-ager who had 15 million followers on Instagram and was now building a business around it. She's mentioned in his book.

He talked about himself. FUBU stands for "For us, by us." He sold clothes into the burgeoning hip-hop community that he had been so passionate about.

• NETWORK

LL Cool J lived down the street but he didn't know him. So he showed up at his house every day and begged him to wear FUBU clothes.

Finally LL did, even wearing one on a Gap video, and in the $30 million video he said the phrase, "For us, by us," while wearing the cap.

"If I had millions of dollars, I would not have begged LL and slowly won him over. I probably would have just paid him and then lost him. Money would've cost me rather than having a mission around what I was doing. I had to get down and BEG LL until it worked."

• OPM

Sometimes it means "other people's money" but sometimes it might mean "other people's mistakes" or "other people's momentum" (the way LL piggybacked FUBU on the momentum he had from the Gap ads).

Learn from other people — mistakes, money, momentum, motivations, whatever it takes. Fill in the M.

• AFFORDABLE STEPS FORWARD

If you sell 800 hats, don't try to sell a million the next day. Sell 1,000. Always take affordable steps forward so you aren't at risk of going out of business.

"Don't take a $200,000 loan out on day one."

But I challenged him on that, which led to this.

• ALWAYS MANAGE RISK

I said, "But your mom mortgaged her house to give you $100,000 for the business. How does that match up?"

He said, "Yeah, but I had an order for $300,000 from Macy's that I had to fill.

"As soon as I had the $100,000, I made the clothes, Macy's paid me, and I paid back the bank. I never would have taken out the loan without knowing in advance how I would pay it back."

I have loaned out a lot of money and I don't think I've ever gotten paid back once. I guess this is why I have gone broke so many times.

People think entrepreneurs take risks. This is not true. Entrepreneurs want to make more money than they spend. Period.

This means ALL of the time is spent on managing risks and costs.

• TESTING

"We were out on the streets selling hats and every day we'd try new prices, new styles, new sizes. We'd see what would work and then double down on what worked and stop doing what didn't work."

Later on I asked him about some of the businesses he invested in with "Shark Tank."

He told me the story of one company and how they would constantly do ads on Facebook for $100 to see what products people would click on. "We would do up to five ads simultaneously and we'd have ads running all of the time."

Whatever people clicked on, those are the products they would sell.

ABT—always be testing.

*   *   *

We talked about jobs. How a job is like running a very small business with one source of revenue.

How the fact that people live paycheck to paycheck because that "personal business" usually just breaks even or even loses money.

"Even when I was starting FUBU, I had two different jobs. I had to make more money than I was spending or it wasn't worth it. We shut down FUBU twice during those first few years but people kept calling us back for bigger and bigger orders and then it was making money."

I asked him what he looked for in a company he invests in "Shark Tank." He's put almost $8 million into companies on "Shark Tank."

"I look at the number of times the entrepreneur has failed," he said. "I don't want them to have their learning experiences on my dime."

"I have to like the person," he said.

This to me is the most important. I've invested in many companies and have had many failures and some successes.

The only successes were when I really liked the entrepreneur. And all of the failures came when I thought the idea was more important than the person.

I said, "I can relate to the 'power of broke'—the grit, the hustle, and so on—but doesn't this glamorize being broke a bit? When I was broke, it was really painful. I felt like I would never get up again. Never live."

He said, "Being broke is temporary but poverty of mind is permanent. You have to avoid poverty of mind."

You can always learn from failures. Take affordable risks. Start fresh even stronger and get back to that hustle.

He said, "I apply the 'power of broke' every single day of my life."

"I don't believe it," I said. "What did you today that was the 'power of broke?'"

"Well," he said, "today I wanted to promote my book as cheaply and powerfully as possible."

"What did you do?"

"I called you."

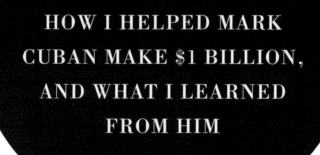

HOW I HELPED MARK CUBAN MAKE $1 BILLION, AND WHAT I LEARNED FROM HIM

Mark Cuban's company, AudioNet (later named Broadcast.com), called me up in 1997 because they desperately needed my help in order for Cuban to become the billionaire he rightfully became.

They wined me, dined me, called me up every day, until finally I granted them their wish.

I don't follow every aspect of Mark Cuban's career. So I'm only going to discuss my own brief interactions with the periphery of his business life to explain what I've learned from him. Suffice to say, he's enormously successful. He had Broadcast.com, which he sold to Yahoo!

And then he sold all his shares at the very top, walking away with billions, which he's probably turned into a billion or so more. He then bought the Dallas Mavericks, started HDNet, made a ton of investments, had a very public battle with Donald Trump, had a very public battle with the SEC, etc.

I called a friend of mine the other day. "Are you jealous of Cuban?" I asked him. And he said, "Of course I am."

Which is good because if he said "no," he would've been a liar. And if he said, "No, that guy just got lucky," he would be the worst personality cocktail out there: stupid and mean.

What I learned from Cuban:

1) CREATE YOUR LUCK

Most people I speak to about Cuban say he was lucky. He created a company with minimal revenues in the Internet video/audio space, had the biggest IPO in history at the time (1998), immediately put the company up for sale, sold to the biggest Internet company (Yahoo!), and then sold all his shares at the very top.

How did he know to sell at the top? Is that the "luck" part everyone refers to? Or the fact that he started a company with no revs and was just "lucky" it was at the right time (the Internet bubble)?

It wasn't luck at all. In chess there's a saying: "Only the good players are lucky."
Whenever a good player wins a game, the angry opponent often says, "Ah, you were just lucky."

But it always seems the good player gets lucky more than the bad player.

People are starved for love and affection. They thrash out everywhere to find it (business, games, relationships, etc.) because they didn't find it as children. And when they see someone else get love (money), they can't understand it. Love doesn't exist, so how did X, Y, or Z get it? It must be luck.

In 1997 when AudioNet contacted me, I had never heard of Cuban.

At the time, my company, Reset, was putting together the first regular live online production of a TV show. "The People's Court with Ed Koch" (a very prestigious TV show if you never watched it) wanted to stream live while it was being filmed. So people online could view it before it went on the air.

I was very excited for several reasons. "The People's Court with

Judge Wapner" was one of my favorites growing up. So now I was seeing from the ground floor how it was being made.

A roomful of production assistants was going through every small claims court case on file. Hundreds or thousands of them. The most interesting ones were being pulled out for airing.

We had our own office right next to this production room, where we would relax between airings. Then, we had a guy onsite every day managing the online streaming. How many people watched online every day back in 1997? Maybe 20? Maybe zero? But it was interesting. And they paid us well.

I also loved being in the Hotel Pennsylvania, where it was being aired, right across the street from Penn Station. It was the site of many New York Open chess tournaments when I had been growing up. So I had fond memories. And also some bad ones.

Anyway, AudioNet contacted us because they were dying for us to use their technology to do the live streaming. I forget the name of their local New York sales person. Very nice guy, persistent.

"Listen," he said. "Mark Cuban wants to go public and we NEED press releases. Press releases drive IPOs. This would be a great press release."

We all laughed about that. We ended up using them.

Mark Cuban understood the game right from the beginning. Create a brand, be at the forefront of technology (but not too far ahead—no electric cars for him), get as many press releases going as possible, sell as fast as you can.

He knew, probably five years in advance, that a bubble was occurring and this was the exact plan to maximize value from it. He probably extracted more from the initial Internet bubble than anyone else. It doesn't happen by luck that you sell at the top. You have to know five years in advance when that top will occur. And then you have to have a very precise plan for being in the right spot at the right time at the very top.

I didn't understand the game. For instance my company was a service business, even though I was developing my own software to build websites. We were streaming many live events. We were doing many things that we could've called "products" and we could've headed down the IPO route by branding our products, speaking at events, etc. I probably had more revenues than half the companies that went public at that time.

But I had no business sophistication at all. All I wanted to do was make payroll, have a little extra (profit) and then sell my business as a function of my profits.

This is fine in most business cycles (it worked) but I didn't maximize the way Cuban did. I don't want to chastise myself but I was right there, right at the same time, and with just as many good products as anyone else. But I didn't properly plan for the events that were occurring (in retrospect) in plain daylight around me.

In other words, I just simply wasn't as smart as Cuban.

Everything is a game. Understanding the rules allows you to succeed.

2) DON'T INVEST IN UGLY

A few years later in 2004, I was starting a fund of hedge funds. I wrote Cuban to see if he wanted to invest. To his credit, he responded and said he didn't like the specific strategy I was using. I was starting a fund of PIPE funds. PIPE funds invest directly into public companies by doing private deals with them so they could get stock at a discount or under other favorable terms.

Companies do this because they need to raise the money and they are incapable of raising money through other means. So, in other words, the worst companies around.

Mark felt the area was ugly and didn't want to be involved.

We wrote back two or three times and each time he responded. I tried to argue with him but he knew where he stood and he remained there. No.

When companies he invested in did PIPEs, he would get out (most notoriously, his back and forth with the SEC over his investment in MAMA and his selling when they did a PIPE).

So what happened? He was right. I smelled the writing on the wall in 2006 and began unwinding my fund before any implosion occurred. The implosion did occur in 2008, two years later, when funds couldn't get out of illiquid positions in microcap companies and they all crashed in the financial crisis.

Mark probably didn't see the exact writing on the wall, but once again he predicted an event that was yet to occur for another four years.

What I learned: PIPEs had a bad reputation even in 2004, but I thought that created opportunity. Mark correctly realized that it's OK to be an optimist in bad situations, but don't be stupid. If you do too many crazy things then you become crazy.

My investors came out OK, but it could've been a lot worse and I should've just listened to Cuban from the beginning.

3) GET COMFORTABLE, THEN GET RICH

Most people think Cuban just stumbled into the dot-com boom, made his billions, and that was that. This next thing I learned from Cuban is critical for any entrepreneur. He had already sold his first software company in the 1990 for $6 million. He could easily have been comfortable for the rest of his life.

That then allowed him the confidence to stretch out his muscles and really go for the billion.

So the rule is, get comfortable, and only then get mega-rich. If you try to go for the big number too early, you can end up miserable.

4) BLEED

Cuban started blogging at blogmaverick.com before just about anyone else was blogging. All over that site you can see stories of his first company, of his thoughts on the Dallas Mavericks, about Broadcast.com, etc. A great resource.

He then used this excitement about blogging to invest all over the space (IceRocket, Weblogs, etc.) and although those were successes, I think he was doing it more for fun than anything.

And he used his blog to keep his name out there in the community. To keep building his personal brand. That's very valuable.

5) CUBAN'S RULES FOR INVESTING

Cuban made his billions and now he does what ever he wants. And pretty publicly. He buys movie chains. He produces movies (because he knows he has distribution for them). He loves basketball (the initial impetus for AudioNet was that he wanted to watch basketball games from his college over the Internet) so he bought the Dallas Mavericks and has probably increased their value by several hundred million dollars.

It seems like there are a few rules Cuban sticks to when investing, going all the way back to the '90s:

1. Find something you are super excited about and know that at least another 100 million people can be super excited about it.

2. Either start a company in that space or invest as much as possible in it. Also, strongly participate in it. Make sure you are the most excited user of your own product.

3. No matter what you are doing, get as much press as possible. Don't use PR firms (maybe he does use PR firms but he certainly doesn't need to; he creates his own PR). Be OUT there creating your own buzz with your own energy. PR firms can never do that for you.

4. Have a good bullshit detector. If things smell, get rid of them. If things are frothy, sell. DON'T BREAK THIS RULE.

5. Engage the customer. Cuban is probably the most accessible owner in the NBA. He talks to the fans. He blogs to entrepreneurs.

In 2004 or 2005, I ran into Jason Calacanis, who started Weblogs, Inc. He told me he cold-called Mark Cuban about his platform and Cuban immediately invested.

Cuban responded to my emails about PIPEs even though he didn't know me and wasn't even interested in PIPES.

It's hard work. I respond to up to 100 emails, comments, etc. a day and still can't keep up. Somehow Cuban has the energy to keep on doing what he's doing, even though he could've long disappeared by now (when's the last time you hear from Todd Wagner, his old partner at Broadcast.com? I'm sure he's doing fine but he's not as public as Cuban).

And yes, I'm jealous. The guy has the dream life. Not everyone can make $1 billion, though. So the challenge then is to make the dream life (or go far beyond what you thought the dream life would've been) by re-calibrating what's really important to you. In my mind, right now, I'm a trillionaire. And getting richer every day.

TEN LESSONS I LEARNED FROM "SHARK TANK"

One friend of mine, who has co-invested with me on two deals, has given me two pieces of advice in life.

One is: "You never know what someone is worth until they declare bankruptcy." Meaning we all speculate that someone is worth $100 million or $1 billion or whatever, and the next day you read in the newspaper that they declare bankruptcy.

Now you know.

The second thing was: "James, you need to watch 'Shark Tank.'"

Since then I've watched every episode, and I can say I agree with him.

For those of you who don't know what "Shark Tank" is, it's the best reality TV show ever. Five investors sit on a stage, keeping them slightly higher than the supplicants who come in asking for money. Then, one by one, aspiring entrepreneurs are led into the "shark tank," where they pitch their products and the "sharks," right then and there, decide whether to give them money.

The entrepreneurs are often humiliated, laughed at, insulted, ask the stupidest questions I've ever heard, but occasionally get some good advice and, even better, walk away with a check if one or more of the "sharks" think their business is a good idea.

The "sharks," as the show describes them, "are filthy rich" and invest their own money.

I'm never jealous of any of these people. Money doesn't buy happiness but it certainly solves your money problems.

It's up to you after that to be happy or not. To avoid self-sabotaging at every opportunity. I can tell you this: I am very good at making money but have a talent for self-sabotage. A talent I have been trying these past few years to suppress.

So I think highly of the people who have learned through experience not to sabotage their successes.

Here's what have I learned from the show. Some items are good for investors, some for entrepreneurs, some for me, and some for my kids.

1. MATH

The first thing that happens when an entrepreneur enters is they say: "Hi, my name is ABC and I'm asking for a $100,000 for 10% stake in my company."
At this point we would pause the show and I'd ask my kids how much the company is worth. Any trader, investor, entrepreneur, does this math instantly and I wanted my kids to get good at it.

And they did. At first the answers (from either kid) would be a nervous: "I don't know." But by the last episode, they were doing it in their heads and blurting it out before I even hit pause.

But sometimes the entrepreneurs would present confusing numbers like, "I'm asking for $85,000 for 15% of my company." And then they'd launch straight into their story. To be honest, I can't even do this accurately and quickly in my head. I always wondered if these entrepreneurs did this on purpose, so that the sharks would focus more on the product than the specific valuation.

2. NOT EVERYTHING IS AS IT APPEARS

This is a TV show. Not a venture capital firm—where, also, by the way, not everything is as it appears. In fact, in all of life, nothing is as it appears but this is never more true than a "reality" TV show.

For instance, in the beginning intro the show says, "Barbara Corcoran took a $1,000 loan and turned it into a real estate empire worth hundreds of millions."

Except she sold her "hundreds of millions" company for $60 million, which they don't say.

I'm not saying she's poor. She's incredibly smart and successful. But the TV show hypes it up. There's subterfuge like that throughout the show.

Kevin O'Leary, who plays it up as the most obnoxious member of the sharks, is described as someone who "built a software company in his garage and sold it for $3.7 billion."

That's true. He built the Learning Company and sold it to Mattel. What they don't say is how much he owned of it (so we can estimate his worth). He clearly made some money on it. But he bought hundreds of companies first. So each company, assuming it was bought in part for stock, diluted his share. So his stake might have been tiny.

And then Mattel repeatedly missed their earnings estimates because of the acquisition of his company. In fact, the acquisition has been described as "one of the worst acquisitions in history" in various articles about it.

But, fair enough. Kevin turned this "success" into having a role at a venture capital firm. I am guessing it's his firm's money (rather than his personal money) that he uses when writing checks on the show.

I went through this exercise with each shark and in every case it was not how they described it on the show (except in the case of Mark Cuban).

My only guidance for the people who are going on the show, or for anyone who pitches any investor, is to carefully study every aspect of the background of the people you are pitching. There are many ways you can use that to your advantage in the actual pitch. And because these guys, in particular, have very public personas, there are a lot of venues you can research their net worth, their successes, their failures, their interests, their distastes, and so on.

3. SELL THE DREAM, NOT THE SALES

Many of the entrepreneurs go in there and say, "I sold $11,000 of this product last year from my garage."

These are the people that get either the worst deals or no deal at all. Nobody cares about $11,000 in sales. Sometimes the sharks don't even care about close to $1 million in sales over the last year. (A great example was games2u.com, which I thought was an excellent company but walked away with no deal.)

And yet some companies with no sales walked away with a great deal. Here is what the sharks (or any investors) want to really understand: Do you have a great product? Do you know what the size of your market is? Do you have some sense of a business model? And, in some cases, do you have big breasts?

How do they know if you have a great product? They can tell by your background, they can tell by the technical expertise you needed to make the product, they can tell if you have a patent, and they can tell if you say, "I have three distributors about to send me purchase orders for the product."

You might not have a dime of sales but if you show that people are interested and that your product is special, you'll get an offer. If you also say, "And for the last three years I've had a total of $53,000 in sales even though I've had a full-time job," then you will definitely not get a deal.

Sell the dream. Better not to have sales unless you are going to blow them away with your sales numbers.

4. DON'T NICKEL AND DIME

It's not so bad to "nickel plus dime," and I'll explain that in a moment. But if you went in there and said, "I'd like $100 for 25% of my company," and you have no sales and one of the sharks says, "I'll give you $100 for 40% of your company," then just say yes. What do you care about the percentage?

As Cuban said in one of the episodes, "Better to have 20% of a $100 million company than 100% of nothing."

With one successful company I sold I wanted my partner to take 10%. Instead they asked for 50%. I gave it to them and sold the company four months later. To them! Because with 50%, they had to care. With 10% maybe they would not have cared.

However, you should nickel plus dime. If Mark Cuban offers you

$100,000 for 30% of your company, push forward and ask for a few more nickels. Price is often the least important part of a negotiation.

Ask him: "Can you introduce me to Netflix?" "Can you get me a promotional deal with the Dallas Mavericks?" "Are there any distributors you can help me license my product to?" Etc.

Get value out of every deal aside from the money. Money won't save or help your business for more than a short time. But the right deal and connections will make or break you. So while they are playing around with the dimes, make sure you collect as many nickels that they may have left lying on the floor.

If you want a deal, then take a deal. Unless…

5. DON'T TAKE THE "HAIL MARY" DEAL

Kevin O'Leary is famous for this deal. He waits for the other sharks to say "I'm out," and then he knows he's the only possibility left for the entrepreneur. So then it suddenly doesn't matter at all what they are asking for.

Let's say the entrepreneur is growing, they have profits, they have one million in sales, etc. Kevin O'Leary doesn't care at all.

Instead, he makes the "hail Mary" offer. Let's say they were asking for $500,000 for 10% of their company, valuing their company at $5 million. Even if the company could be reasonably valued at that, he doesn't care.

He'll say "I'll take 51% of your company for $500,000."

It doesn't matter to him if they say "yes" or "no." If they say "yes," then it's a great deal for him. He just bought control of a company he knows is worth a lot more. If they say "no," then no problem, one out of 10 will say "yes" and he just has to wait it out.

It's the same concept as the story of the guy who wants to have sex so he stands on a street corner and asks every woman who passes him to have sex with him.

Obviously every girl will say "no" to him. Except for maybe one out of 200. He's just standing there waiting for that one. And he'll get it.

Unless it's me. Then it's one out of 3,000.

6. BE THE SOURCE

Kevin O'Leary has two other techniques as a shark that I have to admire, despite his persona as very obnoxious on the show. That persona becomes an asset in various ways because the entrepreneur is instantly trying to get on his good side. But that's not the technique I admire.

One technique Kevin does is he sits there while one or two of the sharks make their offer. Then he asks the entrepreneur to leave the room. Then he turns to the sharks who made the offers and says, "Let's join forces and do this one together."

Then the entrepreneur comes back and, whereas before they had two or three competing offers (an auction environment is always what you want), now they have only one combined offer. They have a minute to decide, and the offer is worse than the lowest offer they had before.

Kevin takes charge of the auction, makes it an "all-or-nothing" deal and again places himself in a "can't lose" situation.

The other technique he uses is to be the source for the entrepreneur. Almost as if they are his friend. Three or four of the sharks might make an offer and compete.

Kevin will then say, "OK, to summarize, here are your four offers." So he's being a source of information. He's "the bank" all of a sudden, seemingly in control of all four offers, and he can spin them in any way he pleases and quiet the sharks who protest because he behaves as if it's a legitimate part of the show.

When you are the bank, it gives you a slight edge over your competitors because the customer wants to do business with the bank.

7. THE DEAL DOESN'T CLOSE UNTIL THE MONEY HITS

Many times the entrepreneur will strike a great deal. He comes in asking for $100 for 10% of his company and he might get $300 for 5% of his company. At the end, the shark who made the deal and the entrepreneur will smile and shake hands (or hug, in the cases when the entrepreneur has big breasts and the shark is a male).

It's all good. Then, in typical Mark Burnett reality show-style, there's the post session interview where the entrepreneur is whooping it up and saying, "Yeah! I just made a deal with the 'Shark Tank'! Yeah!"

My guess is most of these deals don't close. I only have anecdotal evidence. But I looked up several of the companies afterward and there's no mention of their new co-investor. There's only mention of "see us on ABC's Shark Tank this Tuesday!"

One deal, HyConn, got $1.25 million for 100% of his company, from Mark Cuban, with a three-year employment agreement and a royalty. He sold some sort of contraption that made it easy to attach your hose to the faucet or whatever you call it.

But when you go to his Facebook page, he talks about another group of investors and that the deal with Mark Cuban didn't work out. No other details.

Any deal in life goes through several stages: sales, initial questions, the auction (if there is one), the accepted offer, the honeymoon period, due diligence, legal contracts, potential buyer/seller remorse, and then cash getting wired. The TV show only takes us through "the accepted offer," but at any point there's the chance the deal can fail. This is important to remember in any deal at all, including personal relationships.

8. KNOW WHAT YOU ARE GOOD AT

When an entrepreneur first steps through the door, my daughters and I would try to figure out which investor/shark was good for the entrepreneur and we were usually right.

If it was a clothing idea and Daymond John didn't like it, it was all over.

If a product looked like it would be ideal for an infomercial (a pushup machine that makes pushups easier) and the infomercial expert didn't like it, then no deal.

If it was an Internet play and Mark Cuban didn't like it, then no deal.

This is useful to me as an investor. I don't like to think very hard when I invest in private companies. I like to know that investors who are experts in the space of the company are co-investing alongside of me.

In fact, another Kevin O'Leary trick: he would stay silent, but if he saw that the infomercial king was investing, he'd try to get in on the action and partner with him because he knows the infomercial king would make an infomercial, get it on TV, and do all the hard work.

It's also useful to entrepreneurs. Pitch to the right guy. Don't just throw it out there to Barbara Corcoran, the real estate queen, if you have a product that you are going to sell to fire stations.

9. GET ADVICE WHEN YOU CAN

Some of the pitching entrepreneurs simply had bad ideas. If you're selling a pair of jeans, for instance, and Daymond John doesn't want to buy it, then that tells you right there that you probably have a bad idea.

But only once on the show have I heard anyone ask, "What did I do wrong in this pitch?"

And even then, when they gave him advice, he was defensive and insulting to them. If you don't get the deal, learn what you did wrong, and modify your product, modify your approach, or just start a new business. This is not the end of your life if you don't get some crappy deal on "Shark Tank."

10. WHO CARES?

You just presented your product for 15 minutes on a nationally broadcasted TV show that will be re-aired at least two or three times and sell a ton of shows on iTunes. That sort of advertising would cost about $1 million dollars or more. So who cares if you get a deal?

No matter how good or bad the product, it will get a lot of attention and an onslaught of orders. Make sure your website is ready for it, and be thankful for the free publicity. Some of these people were crying when they couldn't get a deal. An entrepreneur takes advantage of every situation and opportunity.

Around $1 million worth of free advertising, plus great advice from a bunch of insulting billionaires, is a great experience for you and your business. Make the most of it.

10

TEN THINGS I LEARNED FROM INTERVIEWING TONY ROBBINS

When we got to Tony Robbins' house we were specifically prevented from photographing his sneakers. I took out the camera but his assistant shook her head "no." Which made me even more feverish to take the picture, but I didn't.

Everyone takes their shoes off. And all the other shoes were like normal human shoes. Then there were his sneakers.

My business partner called me after we did a major deal in 2004. I was about to go broke when we did this deal but we did it and it saved my life.

My partner said, "You'll never guess what number I wrote down in 2001 after we both read 'Awaken the Giant Within,'" and of course I guessed correctly.

It was the number we made in 2004.

In 2001 he was ashamed to tell me.

"Guess who I am reading?" And then we realized we were reading the same books. Both of Tony Robbins books. But they were written so long ago I kept going to the bookstore thinking Tony Robbins was going to have a new book out any day.

But he didn't. It wasn't until 2014 that he published a new book, for the first time in 10 years or so.

The book is called "Money," a topic I sometimes know a lot about and sometimes know nothing about. I ran hedge funds, funds of hedge funds, and have advised many money managers, often people managing billions of dollars.

Tony took it one step further and interviewed the top money managers in the world, how they do what they do. He exposed many of the scams still on Wall Street. He gives simple advice that everyone can follow.

So obviously I bought the book and read it right away. Then when I was finished, I really wanted to pick his brain about it. So I called and asked got an interview and that's how I ended up in Tony Robbins' house.

We spoke for an hour. Here's what I learned from the book and from talking to him. I'm mostly going to leave out the financial stuff. All of that is in the book: the scams, the ways to avoid them, the interviews with the amazing people he spoke with.

Here's what I personally learned.

A) ASK LOUSY QUESTIONS, GET LOUSY ANSWERS

Many people say, "Why did this have to happen to me?" Or "Why did I lose that job when I was good?"

These are lousy questions. You will never get an answer that makes your life better. I get bitter, resentful, angry. And anger is a form of fear. I'm usually afraid I'm going to go broke. And if I go broke, I'm afraid I'll die.

You have to ask good questions. "What can I do to improve?" or "How can I find a better job?" or "How can I be grateful that I lost this job?"

Because inside of every problem is the seed of a "difficult gratitude problem" and it always improves your life to solve those problems.

B) TO MASTER ANYTHING, TALK TO THE EXPERTS

Tony told us about a time when he was 24 years old and he wanted to train members of the military to shoot better.

"I had never shot a gun in my life," he said and laughed in his raspy voice. He was scared he wouldn't do a good job.

So how did he solve this problem? He spoke to five excellent sharpshooters, figured out what they all had in common, and then used that to increase the results of the students in the school by 50%.

C) BRING THE TARGET CLOSER

Specifically, he had every student bring the target only a few feet away. Everyone shot bull's-eyes. Then he moved the target back a foot. Bull's-eyes. Then another foot. And so on.

This is true for everything in life. I look at the example Mark Cuban told me. He didn't just start Broadcast.com and make $1 billion. First he started a bar. Then he started a computer business. Then a hedge fund.

He brought the target very close and then moved it further and further away as he succeeded at each thing.

It reminds me how I taught my daughter to serve in tennis when she was 12. "All you have to do is hit the ball into this huge box." Then when she got 10 in a row, I had her move back a few feet until she hit the base line. Now she's the most consistent server on her team (I'm bragging).

D) LOOK AT GOALS DIFFERENTLY

One time Tony asked people what their goals were. One guy said, "I want to make $1 billion!" At first this would seem like an admirable goal — set it high! There's that horrible saying, "Shoot for the moon, because even if you miss it you'll be among the stars."

But Tony said, this guy didn't really understand his goal.

He broke it down. "Why do you want $1 billion?" And the first answer was, "I want my own plane." Tony told him, "Well a plane costs $100 million and you might only be flying 12 times a year. If you charter a jet for $30,000 an hour then it will take you forever to spend $100 million." So suddenly the guy didn't need $1 billion anymore.

He needed $900 million.

"By the end of that session," Tony said, "it turns out to achieve the exact lifestyle he thought he needed $1 billion for, he needed $10 million." This is still a lot of money but this was Tony's way of bringing the target closer.

E) EXPERTS KNOW THEY KNOW NOTHING

All the time I get spam financial newsletters saying, "The markets are going to zero!" or "This stock is going to go up 1000%!" The reality is the experts know zero. With every investment expert that Tony interviewed they not only had a plan B. They had a plan C, D, and E.

The best professionals in the business admit they know nothing.

Nobody can predict the future. Anything can happen. When I got out of the "future" business I was much happier. I got into the possibility business.

This made me a lot more successful. Leave the future business for the possibility business and the world will get infinitely larger.

F) HIS ENERGY IS INFECTIOUS

Somebody told me he jumps up and down on a trampoline before speaking in front of 10,000 people. He wants his energy at peak.

I thought about doing that before my most recent TED talk but there was no trampoline available. But it's true. When he came downstairs to talk to us he was very excited about the potential for his book to help people. It almost made me want to write about financial stuff again.

After I left his house (and, by the way, that's a BIG house) I had so many ideas about creative things we could do I almost had to pull over and calm down. So I went to Cheesecake Factory and ate until I exploded.

G) THE TONY ROBBINS METHOD

In the interview I said, "OK, I figured it out. You use the Tony Robbins method."

Which I defined as:

* At first you don't know anything.
* You find five people who are the experts in the world.
* You extensively interview them.
* You figure out the simplest things they have in common with each other.
* You do that simple thing over and over and over and over (repetition).

And that's how you succeed.

H) PEOPLE NEED CERTAINTY AND VARIETY

Everyone needs to know where their next meal is coming from. And maybe their next kiss. And maybe… a bunch of things.

We crave some stability, which was the appeal of corporate jobs for the past 100 years (although that period is now coming to an end) and was the appeal of all these mutual fund ads that said, "We return 9% a year."

But most of that stability is a lie. You have to find stability inside yourself first.

For me, it's stable to make money from multiple sources. To know that if I have ideas every day, life will be more stable than if I don't.

But we also need variety. A marriage will die if you stick to the same routine year after year ("the seven-year itch"). A job will get boring. We only have one life. It doesn't mean you quit your marriage or quit your job. But always look for new things to learn. Always look for new ways to surprise. Always look for new ways to break out of your comfort zone.

It's this dance of certainty and uncertainty that makes us human and we often lean too much one way or the other. But if you did that on the dance floor, you'd fall over.

Tony describes this in the book in a financial sense. His goal is to expose the lies in the financial community and get you thinking about how to provide stability there so you can find variety in other parts of your life.

I) SHOW PEOPLE YOU ARE GRATEFUL

When we are very young, we build strong neural circuits across our brains so that electricity can pass quickly between certain neurons. This is why it's easier to learn when we are young than when we are older.

After the age of 20, we lose the ability to "insulate" these neural circuits with myelin, the substance that cements these circuits for life. This is where our basic intelligence comes from. Building as many circuits as possible with myelin protecting them.

I think the same thing happens with relationships. Business, personal, family relationships, etc. They start off young and that's when you can build almost a "relationship myelin" around them. You do that by being honest with people, by showing gratitude, by not overusing the connection, by treating it just right so it develops into something that can last a lifetime.

If someone does something for you, show you are grateful.

J) BE THE SERVANT OF MANY

Tony said in the interview exactly how much he saved in taxes by moving from California to Florida. It was a big number. He had a big house. He's spoken in front of three million people. He's feeding 50 million people. This is a process that took him 30 years or more.

He said the way he did it was by being the servant of many. By constantly adding value to others, value comes back to you. It becomes the most natural thing.

Tony Robbins has his critics I am sure. But I know he helped me get through a hard time 13 years ago, maybe even saved my life. I know he has helped others. People always seem to be afraid to admit it. I know I almost felt ashamed to say I needed help.

But it's by helping others and accepting help that we grow as a society. Sometimes people think "choosing myself" is a selfish concept. But it's the only way you build the strength to help others. It's the only way you surrender, not to some man-made force, but a force inside yourself that is perhaps the most powerful there is.

EINSTEIN'S SECRET
OF PRODUCTIVITY

A producer at [well known television show] said to me, "Whatever you do, don't ever say 'I don't know.' If you say that, we'll never ask you back."

Then, thrust into a dark room, mic'd up, camera pointing at me, the producer in my ear, "anddd...GO!" and six of us arguing about the worst, most obscure issue.

"Can the economy pick up an elephant and throw it into the sun?"

I don't know.

People ask me, "How can you stay informed if you don't read or watch news?"

Other people don't ask. They just say, "And this is what is wrong with society. People like him don't stay informed. If everyone did that we'd go back to the Dark Ages."

We're so conditioned to read from people who pretend to "know" that we forget the beauty of "I don't know."

Marie Curie didn't know why some rocks gave off light. So she discovered radioactivity.

The Wright brothers didn't know how to fly in the air. So they took the science of riding a bike (a bike is allowed to wobble) and added wings and made a plane.

Andy Warhol didn't know what art would stand out against his peers. So he painted a soup can.

Many people don't know when the baby has consciousness and

when it doesn't. So the past 20 years has seen a massive evolution in brain science.

Einstein didn't know what it would be like for a man traveling at the speed of light, looking at a man standing on Earth.

What a weird thing for someone to not know. Einstein said, "The most beautiful experience we can have is the mysterious."

The "mysterious" gave him a simple equation to define all of time and space.

When I interview people on a podcast, I never know. I want to know. These people have such a variety of backgrounds: writers, artists, entrepreneurs, musicians, astronauts, and on and on.

I want to get at their secrets. To peel back the layers. To grasp a little bit of their heart and feast on it.

What was that moment? The moment where they heard the CLICK—where the lock was picked—and they entered that velvet room?

The room that always seems hidden from me and I keep looking for it.

When I begin a relationship, I don't know anything. And I'm insecure. I have to learn to be comfortable with not knowing.

The layers of a person never end. We each just have to decide when we stop peeling. We'll never know what's at the core. How often do we just sit and dwell in not knowing? To be comfortable with not knowing.

Scott Adams, the creator of Dilbert, told me he likes to argue both sides of an intense issue. Then both sides hate him. ("How can you defend the other side?" each side says.)

I'm jealous of the people who seem to know. They walk around confident, they smile, they are sure of their opinions.

They will die comfortably, wrapped snugly in opinions that carried them from birth to death.

After my divorce, I moved back into the Chelsea Hotel in N.Y.C., where I had lived before I got married.

The Chelsea is known for its drug dealers, its artists, its hookers, its people who got lost for a moment or a decade and found themselves at its doorsteps just to ride out the storm.

Everyone there had a story. But nobody would tell it. Everybody was up to something. None of it was good.

We were all broken. Passing our time enough to get bandaged up again to face the real world.

What am I trying to say? I've reached for the sun and fallen to the Earth. I tried to know. I tried to shout, "here I am!"

Every day there's a new question. What can I possibly do to justify why I am alive? Every day, a new answer to explore. Is this it?

Einstein said, "Curiosity has its own reason for existing."

I don't know. I don't know.

20

THE 20 THINGS I'VE LEARNED FROM LARRY PAGE

I visited Google a while ago and, after almost getting arrested, my mind was blown.

First, I wandered into the garage where they were actually making or fixing the driverless cars. When they finally realized I was wandering around, security had to escort me out.

Then I met with a friend high up at Google and learned some of the things Google was working on.

Nothing was related to search. Everything was related to curing cancer (a bracelet that can make all the cancer cells in your body move toward the bracelet), automating everything (cars being just one of those things), Wi-Fi everywhere (Project Loon) and solving other "billion-person problems."

A problem wasn't considered worthy unless it could solve a problem for a billion people.

So now Alphabet is aligning itself with this strategy: a holding company that owns and invests in other companies that can solve billion-person problems.

It's not divided up by money. It's divided up by mission.

I want to do this in my personal life also.

Just analyzing Larry Page's quotes from the past 10 years is a guidebook for "billion-person success" and for personal success.

Here are some of his quotes:

---

1. *"If you're changing the world, you're working on import-ant things. You're excited to get up in the morning."*

To have well-being in life you need three things:

A) A feeling of competence or growth.
B) Good emotional relationships.
C) Freedom of choice.

Being able to wake up excited in the morning is an outcome of well-being.

Feeling that every day you are working on a billion-person problem will give you those three aspects of well-being.

At the very least, when I wake up I try to remember to ask: who can I help today?
Because I'm a superhero and this is my secret identity.

---

2. *"Especially in technology, we need revolutionary change, not incremental change."*

Too often we get stuck in "good enough." If you build a business that supports your family and maybe provides for retirement, then that is "good enough."

If you write a book that sells 1,000 copies, then that is "good enough."

You ever wonder why planes have gotten slower since 1965? The Dreamliner 787 is actually slower than the 747.

That's OK. It's good enough to get people across the world and save on fuel costs.

It's only the people who push past the "good enough syndrome" that we hear about: Elon Musk building a spaceship. Larry Page indexing all knowledge. Etc.

Isaac Asimov wrote classic science fiction like the Foundation series, but it wasn't good enough for him. He ended up writing 500 more books.

Larry Page keeps pushing so that every day he wakes up knowing he's going to go past "good enough" that day.

What does your "good enough" day look like? What's one thing that moves you past that?

*　＊　*

3. *"My job as a leader is to make sure everybody in the company has great opportunities, and that they feel they're having a meaningful impact and are contributing to the good of society."*

Whenever I've managed companies and have had the small opportunity to be a leader, I've judged my success on only one thing:

Does the employee at night go home and call his or her parents and say, "Guess what I did today?!"

I'm not sure this always works. But I do think Larry Page lifts all his employees to try to be better versions of themselves, to try to surpass him, to try and change the world.

If each employee can say, "Who did I help today?" and have an answer, then that is a good leader.

Empowering others empowers you.

4. *"Lots of companies don't succeed over time. What do they fundamentally do wrong? They usually miss the future."*

The stock market is near all time highs. And yet every company in the original Dow Jones market index (except for GE) has gone out of business.

Even U.S. Steel, which built every building in the country for an entire century, has gone bankrupt.

Never let the practical get in the way of the possible.

It's practical to focus on what you can do right now.

But give yourself time in your life to wonder what is possible and to make even the slightest moves in that direction.

We're at maybe 1% of what is possible. Despite the faster change, we're still moving slowly relative to the opportunities we have. I think a lot of that is because of the negativity... Every story I read is Google vs. someone else. That's boring. We should be focusing on building the things that don't exist.

Sometimes I want to give up on whatever I'm working on. I'm not working on major billion-person problems.

And sometimes I think I write too much about the same thing. Every day I try to think, 'What new thing can I write today?' and I actually get depressed when I can't think of something totally new.

But I am working on things that I think can help people. And if you are outside of people's comfort zones, if you are breaking the normal rules of society, people will try to pull you down.

Larry Page doesn't want to be defined by Google his entire life. He wants to be defined by what he hasn't yet done. What he might even be afraid to do.

I wonder what my life would be like if I started doing all the things I'm afraid to do. If I started defining my life by all the things I have yet to do.

✷　✳　✷

5. *"Many leaders of big organizations, I think, don't believe that change is possible. But if you look at history, things do change, and if your business is static, you're likely to have issues."*

Guess which company held the original patent that Larry Page ultimately derived his own patent from, the one that created Google?

Go ahead. Think a second. Guess.

An employee of this company created the patent and tried to get the company to use it to catalog information on the web.

They refused.

So Robin Li, an employee of The Wall Street Journal, quit the newspaper of capitalism (who owned his patent), moved to China (a communist country), and created Baidu.

And Larry Page modified the patent, filed his own, and created Google.

And The Wall Street Journal got swallowed up by Rupert Murdoch and is dying a slow death.

✳ ✳ ✳

6. *"I think as technologists we should have some safe places where we can try out new things and figure out the effect on society."*

A friend of mine is writing a novel but is afraid to publish it. "Maybe it will be bad," he told me.

Fortunately we live in a world where experimentation is easy. You can make a 30-page novel, publish it on Amazon for nothing, use an assumed name, and test to see if people like it.

Heck, I've done it. And it was fun.

Mac Lethal is a rapper who has gotten over 100 million views on his YouTube videos. Even Ellen had him on her show to demonstrate his skills.

I asked him, "Do you get nervous if one of your videos gets less views than others?"

He gave me valuable advice: "Nobody remembers your bad stuff. They only remember your good stuff."

I live by that.

* * *

7. *"If we were motivated by money, we would have sold the company a long time ago and ended up on a beach."*

Larry Page and Sergey Brin wanted to be academics. When they first patented Google, they tried to sell to Yahoo! for $1 million.

ONE MILLION DOLLARS.

When Yahoo! laughed them out the door, they tried to sell to Excite for $750,000.

Excite laughed them out the door. Now an ex-employee of Google is the CEO of Yahoo! And the founder of Excite works at Google. Google dominates.

Money is a side effect of trying to help others. Trying to solve problems. Trying to move beyond the "good enough."

So many people ask, "How do I get traffic?" That's the wrong question.

If you ask every day, "How did I help people today?" then you will have more traffic and money than you could have imagined.

....

8. *"Invention is not enough. Tesla invented the electric power we use, but he struggled to get it out to people. You have to combine both things: invention and innovation focus, plus the company that can commercialize things and get them to people."*

....

Everyone quotes the iconic story of Thomas Edison "failing" 10,000 times to get the electric light bulb working.

I put failing in quotes because he was doing what any scientist does. He does many experiments until one works.

But what he did that was truly remarkable was convince New York City a few weeks later to light up their downtown using his lights.

The first time ever a city was lit up at night with electricity.

That's innovation. That's how the entire world got lit up.

*　　*　　*

9. *"If you say you want to automate cars and save people's lives, the skills you need for that aren't taught in any particular discipline. I know—I was interested in working on automating cars when I was a Ph.D. student in 1995."*

Too often we get labeled by our degrees and our job titles. Larry Page and Elon Musk were computer science majors. Now they build cars and spaceships.

David Chang was a competitive golfer as a kid, majored in religious studies in college, and then had random gopher jobs in his 20s.

The gopher jobs all happened to be in restaurants, so he became familiar with how the business was run.

Then he started probably the most popular restaurant in N.Y.C., Momofuku. A dozen or so restaurants later, he is one of the most successful restaurateurs in history.

Peter Thiel worked as a lawyer in one of the top law firms in N.Y.

When he quit in order to become an entrepreneur, he told me that many of his colleagues came up to him and said, "I can't believe you are escaping."

Escaping the labels and titles and hopes that everyone else has for us is one of the first steps in choosing ourselves for the success we are meant to have.

We define our lives from our imagination and the things we create with our hands.

*　*　*

10. *"It really matters whether people are working on generating clean energy or improving transportation or making the Internet work better and all those things. And small groups of people can have a really huge impact."*

What I love about this quote is that he combines big problems with small groups.

A small group of people created Google. Not Procter & Gamble. Or AT&T.

Even at Apple, when Steve Jobs wanted to create the Macintosh, he moved his small group to a separate building so they wouldn't get bogged down in the big corporate bureaucracy that Apple was becoming.

Ultimately, they fired him for being too far from the corporate message.

Years later, when Apple was failing, they brought him back. What did he do? He cut most of the products and put people into small groups to solve big problems.

Before his death he revolutionized the movie industry, the computer industry, the music industry, TVs, and even watches (watch sales have plummeted after the release of the Apple Watch).

All of this from a guy who dropped out of college after one semester.

Studying the history of Apple is like studying a microcosm of the history of how to create big ideas. Larry Page is recreating this with his new corporate structure.

*　　✻　　*

11. *"We don't have as many managers as we should, but we would rather have too few than too many."*

The 20th century was the century of middle class corporatism. It even got its own name—"The Peter Principle," which says everyone rises to their level of incompetence.

One of the problems society is having now is that the entire middle layer of management is being demoted, outsourced, replaced by technology, and fired.

This is not a bad or a good thing (although it's scary). But it's a return to the role of masters and apprentices without bureaucracy and paperwork in the middle.

It's how things get done. When ideas go from the head into action with few barriers in the middle.

To be a successful employee, you have to align your interests with those of the company, come up with ideas that further help the customers, and have the mandate to act on those ideas, whether they work or not.

That's why the employee who wrote much of the code inside the Google search engine, Craig Silverstein, is now a billionaire.

Where is he now? He's an employee at online education company, the Khan Academy.

---

12. *"If you ask an economist what's driven economic growth, it's been major advances in things that mattered—the mechanization of farming, mass manufacturing, things like that. The problem is, our society is not organized around doing that."*

Google is now making advances in driverless cars, delivery drones, and other methods of automation.

Everyone gets worried that this will cost jobs. But just look at history. Cars didn't ruin the horse industry. Everyone simply adjusted.

TV didn't replace books. Everything adjusted. The VCR didn't shut down movies.

The Internet didn't replace face-to-face communication (well, the jury is still out).

* * *

....

13. *"What is the one-sentence summary of how you change the world? Always work hard on something uncomfortably exciting!"*

....

Not everyone wants to create a driverless car. Or clean energy. Or solve a billion-person problem.

But I have a list of things that are uncomfortably exciting to me.

They are small, stupid things. Like I'd like to write a novel. Or perform standup comedy. Or maybe start another business based on my ideas for helping people.

Every day I wake up a tiny bit afraid. But I also try to push myself a little closer in those directions. I know then that's how I learn and grow.

Sometimes I push forward. Sometimes I don't. I want to get more comfortable with being uncomfortable.

* * *

....

14. *"I do think there is an important artistic component in what we do. As a technology company I've tried to really stress that."*

....

Nobody knows what the definition of art is.

How about: something that doesn't exist except in the imagination, that you then bring out into the real world, and that has some mix of entertainment, enlightenment, and betterment.

I don't know. Something like that.

Certainly the iPad is a work of art. And the iPad has created works of art. And when I first saw a driverless car I thought, 'That's beautiful.'

I'm going to try and put my fingerprint on something today. And maybe it will be art.

✳   ✱   ✳

15. *"The idea that everyone should slavishly work so they do something inefficiently so they keep their job—that just doesn't make any sense to me. That can't be the right answer."*

We've been hypnotized into thinking that the "normal life" is a "working life."

If you don't "go to work," then you must be sick or on the tiny bit of vacation allotted to you each year.

What if everything you did you could inject a little bit of leisure, a little bit of fun into?

I have fun writing, except when I think I have to meet a deadline (work). I have fun making a business that people actually use except when I think about money too much (work).

When you are at the crossroads, and your heart loves one path and doesn't love the other, forget about which path has the money and the work, and take the path you love.

*   *   *

16. *"We want to build technology that everybody loves using, and that affects everyone. We want to create beautiful, intuitive services and technologies that are so incredibly useful that people use them twice a day. Like they use a toothbrush. There aren't that many things people use twice a day."*

What a great idea for a list of the day!

What are 10 things that can be invented that people would use twice a day?

*   *   *

17. *"You need to invent things and you need to get them to people. You need to commercialize those inventions. Obviously, the best way we've come up with doing that is through companies."*

I was speaking to Naveen Jain, who made his billions on an early search engine, InfoSpace.

He also started a company to mine rare earth minerals on the moon.

But his real goal is extra-planetary colonization.

Somehow we got around to the question of why bother having a company in the middle of that. He has billions. He can just go straight for the colonization part.

He said, "Every idea has to be sustainable. Profitability is proof that an idea is sustainable."

✳   ✳   ✳

18. *"You may think using Google's great, but I still think it's terrible."*

K. Anders Ericsson made famous the "10,000-hour rule," popularized later by Malcolm Gladwell.

The rule is: if you practice WITH INTENT for 10,000 hours, then you will be world-class.
He then wondered why typists would often reach a certain speed level and then never improve no matter how many hours.

After doing research, he found that it's because they forgot the "with intent" part. They were satisfied with "good enough."

You have to constantly come up with new metrics to measure yourself, to compete against yourself, to reach beyond your last plateau.

Google is great. But it can be better. Having this mindset always forces you to push beyond the comfort zone.

Once they changed the way typists viewed their skills (by recreating the feeling of "beginner's mind"), the typists continued to get faster.

*   *   *

19. *"We have a mantra: don't be evil, which is to do the best things we know how for our users, for our customers, for everyone. So I think if we were known for that, it would be a wonderful thing."*

Many people argue whether Google has succeeded at this. That's not the point.

The point is: **values before money.**

A business is a group of people with a goal to solve a problem. Values might be: we want to solve a problem, we want the customer to be happy, we want employees to feel like they have upward mobility, etc.

Once you lose your values, you'll lose the money as well. This why family-run businesses often die by the third generation. The values of the founder got diluted through his descendants until the company failed.

I spoke to Dick Yuengling (CEO of D.G. Yuengling & Son, America's oldest brewery and a fifth generation business) about this.

His family found an interesting way to solve the problem. The business is not inherited. Each generation has to BUY the business from the generation before it. To do that, each generation needs its own values, its new way of doing things that keeps the brand fresh and ongoing.

20. *"I think it is often easier to make progress on mega-ambitious dreams. Since no one else is crazy enough to do it, you have little competition. In fact, there are so few people this crazy that I feel like I know them all by first name."*

Our parents have our best interests at heart and tell us how to be good adults.

Our schools have our best interests.

Our friends, colleagues, sometimes our bosses, sometimes government, think they have our best interests.

But it's only when everyone thinks you are crazy that you know you are going to create something that surprises everyone and really makes your own unique handprint on the world.

And because you went out of the comfort zone, you're only competing against the few other people as crazy as you are.

21. *"You know what it's like to wake up in the middle of the night with a vivid dream? And you know that if you don't have a pencil and pad by the bed, it will be completely gone by the next morning. Sometimes it's important to wake up and stop dreaming. When a really great dream shows up, grab it."*

For every article I've ever written, there are at least 10 more I left behind in the middle of the night thinking I would remember in the morning.

I have to beat myself in the head. I. Will. Not. Remember... Must. Write. Down.

It's hard to wake up. And that's the only thing worth remembering. It's hard to wake up.

*   *   *

22. *"I have always believed that technology should do the hard work—discovery, organization, communication—so users can do what makes them happiest: living and loving, not messing with annoying computers! That means making our products work together seamlessly."*

This is a deep question: who are you? If you have a mechanical hand, is that "you"?

Conversely, if you lose a hand, did you lose a part of you? Are you no longer a complete person? The complete you?

If an implant is put into your brain to access Google, does that effect how you view yourself?

When books were invented, memory suffered. We no longer had to remember as much, because we could look things up.

Does that make our brains less human?

I bet memory has suffered with the rise of Google. Does this mean our consciousness has suffered?

When we created fire, we outsourced part of our digestion to this new invention.

Did this make our stomachs less human?

With technology taking care of the basic tasks of our brain and body, it allows us to achieve things we couldn't previously dream of.

It allows us to learn and explore and to create past the current comfort zone. It allows us to find the happiness, freedom, and well-being we deserve.

✳   ✳   ✳

23. *"Over time, our emerging high-usage products will likely generate significant new revenue streams for Google as well as for our partners, just as search does today."*

This is it. This is why Larry Page re-oriented Google into Alphabet.

Don't waste your most productive energies solving a problem that now only has incremental improvements.

Re-focus the best energies on solving harder and harder problems.

Always keeping the value of "how can I help a billion people?" will keep Google from becoming a Borders bookstore (which went out of business after outsourcing all of their sales to Amazon).

How does this apply to the personal?

Instead of being a cog in the machine for some corporation, come up with ways to automate greater abundance.

Always understand that coming up with multiple ways to help people is ultimately the way to create the biggest impact.

Impact then creates health, friendship, competence, abundance, and freedom.
This chapter is so long. I went past 20 things. And believe it or not, I cut it in half.

If I can just wake up every day and remind myself of these quotes by Larry Page, I know I will have a better life.

But this is also why he created Alphabet and put Google underneath it.

To save the world. To save me.

3

MIMI'S THREE STEPS TO MAKE A MILLION

I think I'm in love with Mimi Ikonn. Oh, and also her husband Alex Ikonn. Don't want to confuse anyone!

When I was a kid, I didn't think I would be happy unless I was a "millionaire." Some kids in my school said they were millionaires and they would make fun of anyone who wasn't.

I asked my dad what he was worth. He said $2. Maybe that scarred me so much that I always make sure to have wads of $2 bills on me at all times.

A year or so later his company went bankrupt. So he wasn't worth the same anymore. In his mind, he was worth ZERO.

For the rest of his life he sat in the living room, depressed, and listened to music. When he was a little boy he loved music and won an award.

At some point we all return to what we loved as a child. I suppose that means I will return to comics, Judy Blume, and spying on people.

A few weeks ago I met Mimi and Alex Ikonn. I was insanely curious about them.

How come? Because Mimi makes videos of herself, delivers real value to people, and then makes over $1 million a year because of those videos.

I don't know how old Mimi is. She's much younger than me. She's much younger than my father ever was when I was alive. He would've liked to live her life.

This is a simple chapter. How to make $1 million.

I am absolutely sure the same techniques that worked for Mimi and Alex can work for anyone. I had them lay it out step by step.

A) EMOTIONS

Mimi became obsessed with beauty and hair. She and Alex watched before-and-after videos of women who were getting hair extensions.

"They seemed much happier after getting extensions," Alex said. "Whenever there are strong emotions about something, you know there is an opportunity."

So Mimi started making videos of herself discussing hair and beauty and hair products.

"I never thought I would get more than 1,000 views," Mimi said. "But I loved doing the videos. And I wanted to share my love for the topics with as many people as possible."

Now she has close to 45 million views with almost 700,000 sub-scribers.

B) HUB AND SPOKE

People ask, "How do I get traffic to my blog?" Or "How do I get buyers of my book?" or "How do I get people to follow me on Twitter?"

A lot of it is about loneliness. We sit in our house writing blog posts and then hit "publish." We want our families to love them.

We want friends to love them. And then we want the world to love them.

I'm really just talking about myself. I know when people enjoy things I do, I feel as if I have a family. I'm happy. At least until the next post.

Mimi loved making the videos but needed traffic. So they did the only two-step technique that gets traffic online for anything you want to do. Well, make it a three-step technique.

1. **LOVE:** Know more, love more, express more, bleed more, than anyone else. Was Mimi the only one doing videos on beauty and hair? No. But maybe she put more passion into it.

2. **SPREAD THE LOVE:** Alex would take images and posts and links to her videos and spread them on Pinterest, Instagram, blogs, other sites and have them all point back to her You-Tube channel.

   I call this the "hub and spoke" approach. YouTube was the hub, with a dozen or so spokes reaching out to popular sites that all would link back to the hub.

3. **MAKE MORE LOVE:** No matter what you do, some things will be good and some will be bad. Not every video or post is going to have views. So you do more.

When you do more, several things happen:

* More people find you.
* You rank higher on search.

* You improve.
* People who find you start clicking on your older videos so now they start to get more views.

The "Make More Love" technique always works.

Michelle Phan did 54 YouTube videos before she made a massive hit.

Hugh Howey had already written 10 novels before he published "Wool," which became a massive bestseller. Clayton Christensen applied to NASA for 18 years in a row before they accepted him.

Make more love.

C) 1000 PEOPLE

Note she said she only thought she was going to get 1,000 viewers. The number 1,000 keeps coming up with people who have HUGE audiences.

Kevin Kelly wrote about this in a great post called "1,000 True Fans." He writes about it kk.org. He's also talked about it on my podcast.

Tim Ferriss talks about how he makes sure every one of his posts is going to deliver value to at least 1,000 people.

Of course he delivers much more value than that. But 1,000 seems to be the right number that people who know seem to focus on.

Keep focusing on delivering value to a 1,000, and then they tell two friends and so on, and next thing you know you have a quarter of a billion views, five bestsellers, movies being made about you, you go into space, you own makeup lines, and on and on and on, depending on what it is you love.

D) BUY LOW, SELL HIGH

Alex and Mimi noticed that many of the other beauty videos were talking about a specific brand of hair extensions for women. So they went to my favorite place in the world—the mall.

"We saw these products were priced at $500," Alex said.

"So then we went on Alibaba and saw the same products being sold for $100. We then went to the manufacturers and saw we could buy directly for $50. The exact same products that were being sold for $500."

They borrowed from mom. Borrowed their full amount off of their credit cards. And they placed an order. Then, (I imagine— they did not tell me this) they prayed.

E) SOFT SELL

Mimi talks about many products on her videos. She expresses a radiant, confident personality and discusses everything she is wearing, what her habits are, what products she uses. She NEVER sells anything.

But underneath the video is a link. www.luxyhair.com.

The orders came in one at a time. Then 100 at a time. They sold out of their inventory, paid everyone back, and bought more.

In their very first year (2010) they had over $1 million in revenues. Ever since then they've had more than $1 million a year in profits. Never once using the words "buy this" anywhere.

F) QVC-A

The most successful people have a model for their success. I think that's why I enjoy Peter Thiel's book "Zero to One" so much. Or Peter Diamandis' "Bold." Or Marcus Lemonis' TV show "The Profit."

Each has a different, but very simple, model for how to achieve success or how to judge which companies are successful.

Mimi and Alex developed their own model. They stick with it, and have it to keep jumping from success to success.

Alex explained it to me:

Q. QUALITY: Everything they do is quality. The cameras they use for videos. ("But not overdoing it, because this is YouTube and not television," said Mimi.) The setting they use and how it fits their message. The products, etc.

V. VALUE: Mimi is not trying to sell anything in her videos. She explains what she does and how she does it. She does the research and believes in the products. Rather than asking, she is giving.

"When you give $1 billion in value," Alex said, "you get $1 billion or more back."

C. CONSISTENCY: I read a book about television once by TV mega-executive Grant Tinker. He was Mary Tyler Moore's husband, ran NBC for awhile, and then ran MTM producing such shows as "The Mary Tyler Moore Show," "The Bob Newhart Show," and a dozen other super-hit TV shows.

I only remember one thing in the book. He said something like, "Whenever they changed the time or date of a show, then that show would die. If you moved a show from Tuesday at 8 p.m. to Thursday at 8:30 p.m. then you just lost your whole audience."

Mimi said, "If you are going to put out a video once a week, put it out once a week. Put it out the same day each week if you can. Don't do once a month. Don't do random. Your audience starts to anticipate and look forward to your shows and knows when to expect them."

A. AUTHENTICITY: Mimi only talks on the videos about what she believes in. There's no fluff. There's no pitch. She's exuberant and it shows on each video.

G) LESS

Mimi and Alex were working 80- to 100-hour weeks. They had the money in the bank. They had achieved their goals. They loved what they were doing. But when you hit a lifelong goal you start to ask, "Is that it?"

They got depressed.

Goals are a myth. Our ancestors for 200,000 years didn't have goals. Every day started from scratch: hunt, forage, eat, sex, sleep, wake up to a new day.

Then we were told to find our "goals." And now everyone says, "I'm 17 years old and feel like I've accomplished nothing in life. What should I do?"

Learning to find happiness with less is true wealth.

Ultimately we are the sum of our experiences and not the sum of our belongings. There is nothing wrong with making money but it is only one small part of living a life of comfort, of compassion, of calm.

Mimi and Alex started to focus more on the other things that were important in their lives.

"And you know what happened?" Alex said. "The more we did that, the more money we made."

*   *   *

I really enjoyed talking to them. I am always curious how people make money through a channel like YouTube. Now I know and I think it can be replicated by anyone who is willing to do all of the above.

I'm afraid I don't have a face for YouTube. Or Instagram. And I'm not even sure I have a face for podcasting. But I love doing what I do. And I like having the time to explore other interests and ideas.

And then sometimes I like doing nothing at all. There's nothing wrong with that also.

HOW TO LEARN TO DO THE IMPOSSIBLE

D aniel was tending sheep in Sudan when a bomb blew both his arms off.

When he heard the bombs in the distance he hid behind a tree but wrapped his arms around the tree. A bomb went off near the tree.

His body was safe, but the arms he had wrapped around the tree blew off. When he came to, he said he wished he were dead so he would not be a burden on his family.

He was 12 years old.

I was ashamed to be talking to Mick Ebeling.

Here's why: when I hear the story above I think, 'That's really sad.' I think, 'I wish that hadn't happened to him.' I think, 'I'm glad it didn't happen to me or anyone I know.'

Mick thinks differently. Mick flew over to the Sudan without any knowledge of arms or war or prosthetics. He got together a bunch of experts on 3D printing, prosthetics, mechanics.

He 3D-printed arms for Daniel in a way that had never been done before, cheaper than prosthetics had ever been made before.

Daniel now has two prosthetic arms. He can feed himself. He can help his family again.

I spoke with Mick. I told him I was ashamed to be talking to him because I would not have thought that way.

He laughed and told me his theories on helping people. His company, Not Impossible, takes high-stakes situations where people say, "It's impossible," and figures out how to make them possible.

Here's how:

A) HELP ONE, HELP MANY

He used his experience with Daniel to come up with ideas on prosthetics that could help many people. He helped Tempt One, a graffiti artist who due to ALS became fully paralyzed except for his eyes, communicate again by designing the EyeWriter.

Then Ebeling uses the experiences of helping one to create products that can help many.

B) BRING RIDICULOUS TO ACCESSIBLE

It was ridiculous to get cheap prosthetics to Daniel in the Sudan without any experience. And yet, just a little brainstorming with the right experts led to Daniel's arms. And now the same technology is accessible to anyone.

C) USE STORY

Intel sponsored Mick's efforts. He went to Intel and told the story of Daniel and told the story of how he was already helping Daniel, with or without Intel, and Intel agreed to sponsor the rest of the journey.

For 5,000 years or longer, humanity has driven forward with storytelling. Too many people forget that but the only way to really communicate effectively is through story.

D) EVERYONE HAS PERMISSION

Nobody gave Mick permission to help Daniel. He just did it. Nobody gave him permission to gather a bunch of experts to his house to help figure out how to create prosthetics that everyone said were impossible. He just did it.

Too often we apply for grants. Or we apply to a company. Or we apply to the government. And then we wait. And we wait. And we want that one special person to choose us.

I hate to use my own cliché, but the benefits of choosing yourself is that other people's lives are saved while you avoid waiting for someone else to choose you.

E) "WE ARE ALREADY DOING THIS"

Mick didn't wait to begin. He didn't wait for funding. He didn't wait to figure it all out in advance before he started.

As soon as he committed to helping Daniel, he immediately:

* Found the experts he needed to talk to (free)
* Got them all talking (mostly free)
* Started brainstorming (free)
* Got materials for one set of arms to be 3D-printed (mostly free)
* Began experimenting (mostly free)

Then he went to Intel and others and said, "We're already doing this. Are you in?"

Too many people say, "I have an idea. Now I need funding."

Don't do that anymore. Stop it!

Say instead, "I'm already doing this. Here are the 10 or 20 things I've done so far. Here are the results. Are you in?"

F) CHANGE THE DEFINITION OF FAILURE

People think: go, go, go, go, go, FAIL, stop.

Mick redefined failure.

"We had many failures while trying to figure this out. But each failure was simply a way to show us what we should do, what we could do better. Every time we failed we knew at least one thing we could do better."

G) OPEN-SOURCE YOUR SUCCESS

Even though his company is for-profit, Mick gave away all of the knowledge he learned for free.

Then other people and companies could build better prosthetics, or tools for deaf people, or tools to help people with ALS to communicate.

Then Mick would be able to incorporate those new technologies back into his products.

The end result: more people help with better and better products that are being made cheaper and cheaper.

Too many people try to hold onto ideas, saying, "It's mine!"

But ideas, and the world, get stronger when they are shared and allowed to mate and grow children and the idea babies make the world better.

H) LOOK FOR THE "ADJACENT POSSIBLE"

When Mick started his research, he found someone who had made a mechanical hand. Not the perfect prosthetic hand. But a cheap hand that could grasp items and was functional.

He started with that and then began brainstorming with the inventor and with others about what else was possible, with the mechanical hand as a starting point.

Never start with a blank page. Find all the things closest to what you want to be possible and use those ideas as starting points to find the next generation of possible.

I) START SMALL

Mick didn't help a billion people have better prosthetics. He helped one person.

"If everyone would just help ONE person today then the world will be a better place tomorrow."

In other words, if everyone reading this chapter would help one person today, the world will be a better place.

Always think at the end of each day, "Who did I help today?"

J) STAND NEXT TO THE SMARTEST PEOPLE

Mick didn't know anything about prosthetics. But he knew that if he brought together the man who made the cheap, mechanical hand, with experts in 3D printing, with experts in prosthetics, then something good could happen.

Even if you aren't an expert, give yourself permission to be a producer. Produce!

After our conversation, Mick and I took a walk and I told him stuff.

"How are you dealing with that?" he asked me.

I said, "Every day I follow my own advice. I try to be healthy. I spend time with friends. I'm creative every day. And I look at the most difficult part of my situation every day and find things to be grateful for.

"This has been amazing for me to see it work in action for myself. I bounce back stronger every day and I feel like life is amazing."

"You should write about that," he said.

I will. I said, "Selfishly, I help one — me, to help many. "

He laughed at that. And we shook hands and then I went one direction and he went to save the world.

10

THE 10 THINGS I LEARNED
from
RICHARD BRANSON

Once I went out at night and fell asleep on a park bench near the beach in Miami.

When I opened my eyes I pretended I had just landed on the world. I knew nothing. Now I had to learn everything.

That's the way I should've been when I was younger. Maybe I would've avoided many problems if I just realized I knew nothing.

ALL SUCCESSFUL PEOPLE started off knowing nothing.

They studied the people who came before them. Who studied the people who came before them. And so on.

I really admire Richard Branson. He's one to study.

Richard Branson is the perfect example of "Ready. Fire. Aim." He starts something. He does it. Then he looks to see if he hit the target. If not, he starts something new.

I love the story of how he started Virgin Airlines. He was already successful from Virgin Records. Note that now he has nothing to do with Virgin Records.

I don't even know if Virgin Records still exists. All that is left is Virgin Airlines.

A flight had gotten cancelled. Everyone was upset.

But Branson wasn't upset. He found a plane that would take him. But he didn't have the money.

One good thing to start with is to always imagine the obstacles gone. Imagine, 'If I wasn't worried about money, would I still make this trip?'

I call this IDEA SUBTRACTION. Subtract the perceived obstacles to an idea and BAM! You find that many more ideas are born from that.

First, he arranged to rent the private plane, even though he still had an obstacle (no money).

Then he put up a sign: "$29 for a plane to Puerto Rico." And everyone signed up. Suddenly he had the money for the plane.

That was his proof-of-concept for an airline. Now that is his main business and it's worth billions.

Here are 10 quotes from him that I think are valuable:

....

1. *"Listen more than you talk. Nobody learned anything by hearing themselves speak."*

2. *"Start making suggestions for how to improve your workplace. Don't be a shrinking violet, quietly getting your job done adequately. Be bold, and the sky is the limit."*

....

Note he's not suggesting starting a company. You can always create inside ANY surrounding and you will be infinitely rewarded for that.

The first employee at Google is now a multi-billionaire even though nobody knows his name (Craig Silverstein). He was an employee and he created and blossomed.

---

3. *"Age isn't as important so long as you are surrounded by people you love, doing things you passionately believe in."*

I truly believe this. We all have things we love to do. And it's the people around us who love us that help us unlock these dreams.

It's ONLY when you find the people you love that you can create and flourish. Henry Ford was 45 when he started his third car company and created the assembly line. He did this once he eliminated all the people who tried to control him at prior companies.

Colonel Sanders was 65 when he started KFC.

Laura Ingalls Wilder was 65 when she wrote her first book. The book launched the Little House on the Prairie series.

This was after she had been totally wiped out in the Great Depression and left with nothing but she started to surround herself with people who encouraged her and pushed her to pursue writing to make ends meet.

---

4. *"What humanity has collectively learned so far would make up a tiny mark within the circle. Everything we all have to learn in the future would take up the rest of the space. It is a big universe, and we are all learning more about it every day. If you aren't listening, you are missing out."*

The other day someone asked me if I believe in God. There's no answer. Always have reverence for the infinite things we will never know. Our brains are too small.

This next quote I slightly want to change:

....

5. *"To be a real entrepreneur you always have to be looking forward. The moment you rest on your laurels is the moment your competition overtakes you."*

....

I think "entrepreneur" can be changed to "human." We all have to survive and succeed first as humans. And the job description changes every day.

Every day there is room to finish this sculpture that began the moment our mothers released us into the world.

....

6. *"There is no such thing as a boring person: everyone has stories and insights worth sharing. While on the road, we let our phones or laptops take up our attention. By doing that, we might miss out on the chance to learn and absorb ideas and inspiration from an unexpected source: our fellow travelers."*

....

Every day has stories hidden inside of it, like a treasure hunt. When you find those stories, you get rewarded. Not by money, but by... I don't know. Something. You feel it when it happens.

7. *"It can be easy to find reasons not to do something. However, you might be surprised by how much help is at hand if you put yourself out there and commit to a project. It doesn't have to be a case of struggling along by yourself."*

We live in a world of connection. The barriers we've erected by storytelling (religion, nationalism, corporatism) are breaking down.

You can crowdsource a revolution with a single tweet now. There are a million ways to ask for help and a million people who want to help you.

But it's hard to ask. There are the old fears of rejection. Fears of people viewing your asking as weakness. Fears of infringing on someone by asking.

Offer value in your ask and then the reasons to not do something start to go away, until there are none left.

And again, Branson is referring to "idea subtraction," which has constantly propelled him from success to success.

8. *"When most people think about taking a risk they associate it with negative connotations, when really they should view it as a positive opportunity. Believe in yourself and back yourself to come out on top. Whether that means studying a course to enable a change of direction, taking up an entry-level position on a career ladder you want to be a part of, or starting your own business — you'll never know if you*

don't give it a try."

....

Another example of how Branson would use "idea subtraction" to come up with tons of ideas.

For instance, sometimes people say, "If only I knew how to program I could do X." Well, imagine you could program. Subtract that worry. Now what ideas would you implement?

You can always subtract a worry. Whether it's putting up a sign ("$29 to get to Puerto Rico") or, as Branson suggests above, taking an entry-level position.

When I started my first successful company my job title was junior programmer analyst at HBO and I had $0 in the bank.

I took an entry-level job so I could move to N.Y.C. and start making connections. I stayed at that job for three years while building my network.

For more than half of those three years I had my first company on the side, building up.

I was afraid all the time I would get caught doing two jobs at the same time.

But I did learn that these almost insurmountable obstacles were the EXACT reason I had huge opportunities.

When people think a problem is impossible they value it at zero. Successful people buy ideas low (zero) and sell them high.

You ask, "Why can't I?" See the following quote from Branson:

9. *"I've always had a soft spot for dreamers—not those who waste their time thinking 'what if' but the ones who look to the sky and say 'why can't I shoot for the moon?'"*

Does he really mean the moon here? Or does that sound cliché? Let's look.

When Branson was a teenager and started his first magazine devoted to music, I doubt he was thinking about shooting for the moon.

But who knows? Now his biggest investment is Virgin Galactic. That magazine (which he started despite severe dyslexia) literally turned into a company that is now shooting to land a ship on the moon.

Why not? Why not?

10. *"Together we can make the products, services, businesses, ideas, and politics for a better future. In this 'new power' world, we are all makers. Let's get making."*

Sometimes people write me and say, "Not everyone is cut out to be an entrepreneur. Some people like being employees."

I agree with this. There is nothing wrong with being an employee. It's what you make of it.

I've been an employee many times. The key is to realize that an "employee" doesn't mean you give up on creating, on making, on coming up with ideas.

In fact, an employee often has more opportunity for abundance than an entrepreneur. The playing field is much larger in a big corporation where everything is possible.

I went to graduate school with Astro Teller. He runs the special projects division at Google, previously called Google X but now just called X. He's an employee at Google.

He was asked to "dream" at Google and now Google, a software company, is making driverless cars. It seems insurmountable: "What if we can make a car without a driver?" But that's where the opportunity is.

Every day I wake up and it's a constant battle in my brain against obstacles. Usually not business obstacles but emotional ones. Fears. People. Ideas. Hopes. This is life. A stream of obstacles and fears in a tough world.

I wish I had paid attention to the many wonderful virtual mentors, the Richard Bransons of the world, when I was younger.

To simply admit "I don't know" and reap the benefits of curiosity.

I hope I learn something today. If not I'll go back and reread these quotes and maybe sleep on a park bench.

GO DOWN THE RABBIT HOLE OF OUR INTERESTS: A LESSON FROM MALALA

Malala was shot in the face for standing up for her beliefs. Her persistence and bravery forced the world to listen. She became the youngest Nobel Peace prize winner in history.

Her inspirations: Martin Luther King. Nelson Mandela.

Nelson Mandela was in jail for 27 years and then saved a country.

Mandela and King's biggest inspiration? Gandhi.

Gandhi created a country by sitting and starving.

The alpha person does not need to shout and fight. The alpha person knows the secrets of radiating power with no movement at all.

Gandhi's influence? Leo Tolstoy.

Tolstoy's "War and Peace" is one of the bestselling books of all time, with over 40 million copies sold.

Personalizing the horror of war, the epics of country and family, and showing the imprints these high-stakes events have on individuals is the universal theme Tolstoy ties into.

We all suffer. But we must all transform that suffering into the art and energy that drives us to change.

Tolstoy's biggest influences? Later in life he lists Buddha, Lao Tzu and stoic philosopher (and slave) Epictetus as his "enormous" influences.

People think Buddhism and Taoism are religions. They aren't. Buddha and Lao Tzu never mention a god.

They mention:

1. Suffering will always happen.
2. Suffering will cause you to react.
3. You can remove yourself from the suffering by noticing your reaction instead of being a slave to it. Too often we are slaves to fear instead of masters of growth.
4. Noticing your reactions to suffering, anger, pain is the key to well-being.

For instance, when someone yells at me, I often can't help myself: I get angry. I want to yell. I want to fight.

If a boss is cruel, I feel bad and afraid and angry. If a friend insults me, I get defensive and afraid. If I lose money, I panic.

It's important for me to notice: something inside of me wants to react.

I'm not always good at this. Sometimes I react too fast. Before I notice. Before I take a step back. Before I am calm.

I have to give myself permission to not be as good as I can be. I have to practice. Practice, for me, creates greater calm and then maybe happiness.

All of this is to say, follow down the rabbit hole of your influences. Every song you like, every movie, every book, every leader, every philosopher.

The seeds of change were planted a long time ago. Centuries ago. Follow the path.

Read them. Study who they read. Wonder about their ideas. Wonder about their history.

Every day I try to jump down that rabbit hole. I find something I love. I dive in. Where did that love find its roots?

It's fun. You'll learn. Life will get better no matter how bad it seems now.

It will always be better when you explore the rest of the iceberg you are just sitting on the top of.

People say, "What do you wish you knew as a kid?"

The trite answer: "Nothing." Else I would not have experienced all the misery and depression that brought me to this moment.

The real answer?

This.

This moment when I fell in love with something—a person, a quote, an action, a work of art. And I jumped down the rabbit hole.

This chapter that I wrote above. This piece that I started with, "Malala was shot in the face…"

DO YOU MAKE FEAR DECISIONS OR GROWTH DECISIONS?

I was afraid I was going to lose my biggest client. And my job. So I let him yell at me. Repeatedly.

I met a friend of mine. She said, "My grandma told me there are only two types of decisions: decisions made out of fear and decisions made out of growth."

For instance, do you stay in your job because you are afraid you won't get another job? Or do you stay in your job because you are excited about the growth potential there?

Do you stay in a relationship because you are afraid you won't meet someone else, or you are afraid it will be bad for your kids, or you are afraid of hurting someone else?

Or do you stay in a relationship because you are truly grateful the other person is in your life? (And hopefully vice versa.)

I thought about it. I looked at all my major decisions in my life.

* Moving to N.Y.C. for HBO
* Leaving HBO to start a company
* Getting married and having kids. Getting divorced.
* Moving 80 miles out of N.Y.C. after losing home and money.
* Getting married and divorced the second time.
* Trying to sell a company before it had fully bloomed.
* Not taking business trips because I was nervous about what would happen if I left home.

And on and on. My friend's grandma was right!

Every decision I have made has either been fear or growth. Not just big decisions but even the smallest decisions.

And the fear-based decisions never worked out for me. When I made a fear-based decision it was always because I was giving power to someone else.

I'd make a fear-based decision out of insecurity. Out of a feeling of scarcity. Out of giving too much power to others so they would control my life.

The growth-based decisions all resulted in miracles I could not have imagined.

With growth-based decisions you feel it in your body: an expansion of your chest, ideas in your mind, a feeling of competence increasing. A feeling of freedom expanding.

A growth-based decision becomes the story of your life later. A fear-based decision turns into regret.

In fear-based decisions, you feel it in your head. I better do this... OR ELSE. I listened to one of my first bosses yell at me so many times because I was afraid he would fire me if I argued.

I didn't want to get fired because I had a company on the side and HBO (my job at the time) was the biggest client. I had no confidence in my company. So fear of losing a client prevented me from devoting all of my time to the real growth in my life

One time I was scared I was going to go broke again. So I took a job. I tried to convince myself that it was a growth decision. Maybe I would expand at the job and create opportunities.

But the first day at the job I fell straight to the ground for no reason.

Everyone laughed and said, "Are you OK?" and I got up because I was ashamed and embarrassed at all the people looking at me.

I started to limp because I hurt my leg so badly.

The second day at the job, the boss of the company told me, "Trust me on your salary. We'll take care of you."

And I was afraid to argue. He was the boss.

The third day at the job, I got up and walked out. I didn't clean out my office. I left my jacket there. I took the elevator down 40 stories. I walked out into the sun. And I never went back.

They called repeatedly. Even a year later the main guy was still calling.

My life is better than ever. I never looked back. I left the building and walked to Grand Central. I took the train 80 miles. I watched the leaves turning from green to red along the way across the Hudson River.

I came to my house and walked the one block to the river and breathed in the air, not knowing how, what, why. Not thinking about money for the first time in months.

And then I noticed. I wasn't limping. My leg didn't hurt.

Not everything went well for me after that decision. Some pretty awful things happened. My heart tore open more than once. My fears about money came back again and again.

But it was a growth decision. And bit by bit, the growth decisions added up. And bit by bit, I grew to love my life more than I ever had.

Thank you, my friend's grandma.

DARE OF THE DAY

S he said, "I am an introvert but had to develop tricks to fake being an extrovert because of where I worked."

I said, "Do you think everyone in L.A. is an extrovert?"

She said, "I don't know. Maybe they are all faking."

We were at a party. I had been sleeping but a friend called me up and said, "You have to go this party three blocks away from you." So I did.

Why? Because why not? Sometimes you know to say no. But to surrender to the moment, if nobody is getting hurt, sometimes you say yes. I went.

It was crowded and I knew some of the people and other people I didn't. I didn't know her but we were introduced.

"You have to ask her for [X] favor," the introducer whispered to me. But I never got around to the favor.

I said, "Can you tell me some of the tricks?"

I asked because sometimes I feel I don't really know how to live and look like a normal person.

Sometimes I like being home and writing and reading all day because that passes for human without me having to see, or touch, or talk to anyone. When I go outside, I often feel unhinged. Like I could float away.

So I wanted to know.

She didn't tell me at first.

"Please."

"OK," she said. "Sometimes I would do what I call a 'dare of the day.' I would do something that I might be scared to do or was out of my comfort zone."

"Like what?" I asked.

She didn't want to tell me.

"Please."

She squinted her eyes at my face then touched my cheek and rubbed her fingers together as if pulling something off my face.

"I would go up to people, strangers, and pretend to pull a wisp of hair off of their face."

"That would freak me out," I said. Both doing it and having some stranger touch my face.

"I would do all sorts of things like that."

"OK," I said, "I want to try this. Start me off. Tell me more or tell me what I should do tomorrow."

"I can't."

She made a motion with her fingers around her head the way people do when describing someone who is crazy.

She said, "Now that I've told you this, your mind will start working on it. Tomorrow you will wake up and your body will know what to do."

She told me the rest of her story, which was fascinating. Then I went home.

I woke up and I was upset about something that had happened earlier the day before.

My friend Amy had advice: "Go and eat pancakes and bacon and photograph it so I know you are eating. You have to prove it to me."

I went. I ate. I photographed.

Then my body knew what to do.

I walked outside and there was a man and his daughter. I held up my hands with palms out, non-confrontational and said, "Good morning!" and they smiled and said good morning back.

I started walking home. I saw a couple holding hands. Palms out. "Good morning! And you (the girl), I love your blue hair. And you (the boy) I love your jacket."

A pretty girl crossed the street. "Good morning!" She angled away from me as she walked past. I guess it might be taken the wrong way sometimes. Maybe it might not be attractive.

"Good morning!" I said to a guy opening up his store. He smiled.

"Hey, good morning, guy."

I said it all the way home. I got home. I didn't feel down any-more. The sun was coming in. I started to write.

First I wrote the girl from the party and told her what happened.

She wrote back (I'm going to paraphrase), "Don't record your dares. That's why I was hesitant to tell you the dares I did."

OK, other than this one, I won't.

She said, "It will take a few weeks to figure out your boundaries on dares. Both personal and physical."

She said, "Don't dare anyone else to do this."

I didn't understand her reason. But maybe it would affect the way I did my own dares. SO DON'T DO THIS.

I wanted to leave the party but I had one more question.

"What did you do after you were working in L.A. for so long as an assistant?"

She said, "I went to get a Ph.D. in robotics at [best school in world for robotics]." She laughed and I think she said, "Maybe that was a dare for myself also."

I went home. I went to sleep. And she was right.

My mind was going crazy that night. But in a good way.

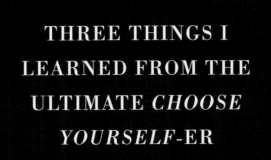

3

THREE THINGS I LEARNED FROM THE ULTIMATE *CHOOSE YOURSELF*-ER

Your dad is an alcoholic. Your mom is mentally ill from syphilis and is institutionalized when you are a child.

You quit school at the age of 13 and essentially join the circus to pay the bills. And ever after, you have to make people laugh to get paid.

You move to Hollywood and after some success you ask for a raise from the movie studio you work for. They refuse you because... that's what bosses do.

Then you go to another movie studio, make some successful movies, ask for a raise... and they hate you.

No family, no education, bosses that will consistently try to screw you.

So Charlie Chaplin chose himself. With Mary Pickford, Douglas Fairbanks, and D.W. Griffith, they formed United Artists, which became one of the biggest movie studios in Hollywood history and also the first studio formed by actors.

They chose their own movies, they created their own success, they picked their scripts, they paid themselves out of profits, which were substantial. Nobody could stop them. They had freedom. They became the most highly paid actors in the world.

And they enjoyed doing it.

Chaplin kept increasing his competence, both as an actor and as a screenwriter, a director, a composer, a businessman, and all aspects of the movie industry. Every day he focused on his freedom so he could never again be beholden to the people who tried to keep him down, even his fans who often hated him or doubted him. Even the U.S., which often was suspicious of him and even banned him. Even the directors and industry that loved him—he never let that love entrap him.

Everyone wants the keys to your self-esteem so they can lock you in your own jail.

Success doesn't mean money if it causes misery.

Success is every day, feeling contentment.

Contentment is every day:

* Improving your relationships
* Improving your competence in something you love
* Improving your freedom

Today I spoke with old friends. I wrote and tried to be creative. I'm improving my relationships with business associates.

I don't think this out of fear. I do this because it's how I grow. When I fail to do this, I lose all my money. I lose all my friends. And I lose my self-respect.

I tell my friends, "If you ever see me in the gutter with a needle, please help me."

Nobody has ever helped me. I have to pull the needle out.

I learn from Charlie Chaplin to take control of every aspect of my creativity and freedom. The jail keepers can never be trusted with my freedom. Only I can.

Charlie Chaplin left us with three great quotes that show he had the *Choose Yourself* mentality.

I think about these three quotes that have resonated through time to land right here and how they apply in my life now:

1. *"Nothing is permanent in this world, not even our troubles."*
   Eventually, if I keep increasing my well-being and competence with the three things I mentioned above, I have always gotten out of the gutter.

2. *"I like walking in the rain, because nobody can see my tears."*
   I have to give myself permission to be sad. The last time I cried was... yesterday. And it washes away and a new day begins.

3. *"A day without laughter is a day wasted."*
   The end of last year and the beginning of this year was a difficult time for me. The only thing that saved me was laughing as much as possible.

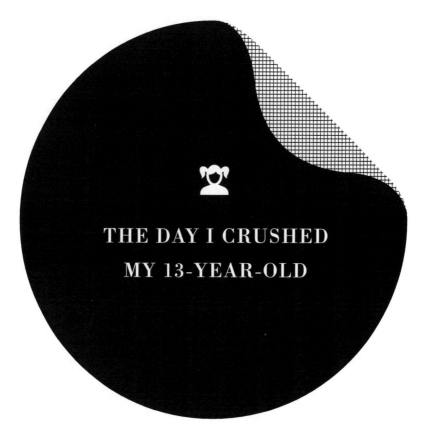

THE DAY I CRUSHED
MY 13-YEAR-OLD

When my daughter was 13, I'd take her to play tennis once a week and I'd crush her and she'd cry.

She's gotten a lot better at tennis since then, and it's not as easy for me to beat her. I thought this would probably happen, so I took the opportunity while I had it.

Sometimes I'd hit the ball as hard as possible so she couldn't run fast enough with her tiny legs.

Other times I'd aim straight at her so the ball would either hit her ("ow!") or she had to jump out of the way.

Sometimes she'd yell, "I hate tennis!" and then cry.

I don't know why, but when we got to that point I'd feel happy.

Because then I could comfort her.

*　　✴　　*

Some people told me, "Let the kid win sometimes."

I don't like to do that. When my dad used to do that to me I could tell. I would throw the racket at him. Or I would throw the pieces off the chessboard. I was 21 years old.

There are two ways to learn: passively and aggressively.

Passively is when you study your mistakes, read the history of what you are learning, network, find your "tribe," find a mentor, etc.

Aggressively is right when you are in the middle of it. You're neck deep and the ball is coming at you: what do you do?

Passively is in your head. Aggressively is noticing RIGHT NOW and taking action.

In your head is important. But ACTION is what creates heroes.

*   *   *

One time I was thrown right into the middle of a huge multi-million-dollar line software project. We were programming Time Warner's "interactive TV" experiment in Orlando.

Now everyone just turns on their Apple TV and starts streaming. Think of this as the first version of that. I had no clue what I was doing and I had to learn fast or be fired.

In my arrogance I suggested to my boss that Time Warner should use "the Internet" to deliver video to customer homes. This was in 1994.

My boss said, "James! The Internet is great for academics. But these cable guys know what they are doing. Trust that they know better than you."

So I had to learn all of these programming techniques very fast (or I would be fired) that ended up helping me for many years after.

Another time I was CEO of a company that was about to miss payroll. I would wake up in the middle of the night adding up numbers to see if we would make it. If we would survive. If I would survive.

I had never sold anything in my life. I had to learn how to be a salesman very quickly or we wouldn't meet payroll.

I don't know if I did a very good job at it. But I had to learn very fast so at least I wouldn't be bad at it. I'm still learning.

In the past 30 years of teaching people and also learning things under pressure I have found the best AGGRESSIVE technique to learn something very quickly.

Here it is:

THE BRUCE LEE TECHNIQUE

Bruce Lee said, "I don't fear the man who has practiced 10,000 kicks. I fear the man who practiced one kick 10,000 times."

Mollie was having trouble using her backhand to return a serve.

So I bought 200 tennis balls and had her stand on the left side of the court. I served 200 times to the left side of the left box.

Over and over. We didn't rally. As soon as she hit back, I served the next ball. Maybe a little harder or with more spin.

She returned maybe 5% of them and started crying. "I'm horrible!" she said.

"Don't worry," I told her. "Your brain is what learned today but your body learns when you sleep."

So the next day we did it again. And guess what? She returned about 60% of the balls. She was smiling the whole time. "I got better!" she said.

"Don't worry," I told her. "You're going to get worse also."

"Don't be sad when you fail and happy when you succeed. Both are going to happen again and again at every new level."

If we had just played games, she never would've gotten enough experience using her backhand to return a serve. Now she's a much better tennis player.

When I was learning chess, my instructor would put two pawns and a rook on the board versus his rook and told me to try and beat him.

Then he put the two pawns in a different part of the board. Then a different part of the board. For four hours just two pawns and a rook versus a rook.

Did I learn how to win with a rook and two pawns? Maybe.

But I also learned a little more of the subtleties of what a rook is good for. Or which pawns might be ever so slightly more import-ant than other pawns. Or the power of the king when few pieces are left on the board. Or the power of my brain calculating many moves ahead when only a few pieces are on the board.

Sunlight doesn't just hit you. When you open the window, the sunlight hits everything in your house.

When you open the window of learning, you don't learn just the specific thing you are trying to see. You begin to see everything that is now lit.

The real art is paying attention to all of the things you can now see. Now that the sunlight is pouring in.

LESSONS I LEARNED
FROM PLAYING POKER FOR
365 STRAIGHT DAYS

I spent 365 days straight playing poker in 1998-1999, including the night my first kid was born. Including my birthday and my anniversary. Including Christmas and Easter and whatever Jewish holidays occurred during this time.

I used to play at the Mayfair Club on 24th Street and the Diamond Club on 20th Street, both illegal clubs. The Mayfair would close at 4 a.m. and some stragglers would head over to the Diamond, which never seemed to close. Ultimately Giuliani closed both down permanently.

I had a house in Atlantic City and would play there on the weekends. I'd go via helicopter Fridays at 5 p.m. and fly back on Sunday night. Occasionally I would go to Las Vegas and play. This was pre-Internet poker, TV poker, and pre the big money that is in poker now.

The only time life had any color in it for me during this period was when I was sitting around a table, chips in front of me, cards getting dealt, and guys with nothing else in their lives making jokes back and forth while everyone tried to take everyone else's money.

Poker sucks. Here's why:

A) EVERYONE AT THE TABLE IS YOUR FRIEND BUT THEY ARE ALL LYING TO YOU TO STEAL YOUR MONEY.

I wanted to be around these grubby guys more than I wanted to be around my wife and newborn. More than I wanted to be around real friends. More than I wanted to be around my work colleagues or my family. I don't know why. Something was wrong with me. All day long I read books about poker, and all night I would play.

I felt for the first time in years like I had a group of "buddies." Like I was one of the guys.

Here's the problem. We all were buddies but we spent the entire night lying and trying to take money from each other.

You could think, "Oh, it's just a game." But I watched some of my friends go broke and cry and borrow and beg and steal. Nobody liked losing all of their money. I watched lawyers get disbarred trying to steal enough money to play poker. I saw guys escape to Israel to avoid extradition when they lost their IRS money to the poker table.

And nobody really cared about them. A guy would stop showing up and then he would be forgotten. Nobody really cared about me. We were friends. Until we weren't. And that was that.

B) IF YOU FIND YOURSELF PLAYING A GAME ALL DAY—ANGRY BIRDS, OR POKER, OR CHESS—ASK YOURSELF: WHAT MIGHT BE WRONG IN MY LIFE?

I was happy I had sold my business, but maybe I wasn't happy working for a boss now. Or maybe I wasn't happy in marriage. Or maybe I wasn't happy that all of my friends were work-related and I had lost every other friend.

An addiction is a symptom. Find the real genetic roots of what is going on.

By the way, not every game player is an addict. Some people make a good living at these games. You have to judge for yourself whether you are a professional or an addict. The professionals win money from the addicts who win money from the amateurs.

C) IN POKER, YOU WANT TO SIT IMMEDIATELY TO THE LEFT OF THE DUMBEST, RICHEST PERSON AT THE TABLE (THIS GOES FOR ALL SORTS OF WAYS TO MAKING MONEY).

He bets, then you raise, no matter what is in your hand. Then everyone else is out and it's just you and him. In the long run you get all his money. This applies to every business endeavor.

D) POKER IS A SKILL GAME PRETENDING TO BE A CHANCE GAME.

Many things in life are like that: sales, negotiating, entrepreneurship, etc. All of these things have the element of chance in them but the ones who are skillful will take all the money from the ones who aren't.

The problem is, most people think they are good because it's hard to rank yourself, and many people go into denial when they lose money. They tell people, "Oh, I broke even," when they lost money most of the night.

Here's how you get better at any skill game:

* Read as many books as you can that were written by players better than you.
* Study hands and the analysis of those hands.
* Study and think about your mistakes. Don't regret your mistakes. You'll always make mistakes. The better you are, the fewer mistakes you make. The only way to get better is to thoroughly analyze your mistakes. So the more mistakes you have, the more opportunities you have to get better. Of

course, this applies to everything you do in life.

* Talk to people smarter than you. Try to learn from them anything you can.

E) IF YOU HAVE A BAD HAND AND SOMEONE RAISES YOU AND SOMEONE THEN RAISES HIM, YOU'RE MOST LIKELY GOING TO NEED LUCK TO WIN. BACK OUT AND TRY AGAIN LATER.

There's a theory in programming chess computers that applies to other areas of life, including this one. It's called "conspiracy theory." If too many things have to happen in order to bring about the situation you want, then back out of it and try again later.

For instance, if you are in love with a girl but she has three kids, is unhappily married, and lives 5,000 miles away, then at least three things have to conspire simultaneously for you to ever end up with that girl.

In poker, if you are facing two potential hands that are better than yours, plus you have to wait for two more rounds of betting to occur (where you can lose more money), and you are waiting for very specific cards that are unlikely to arrive, then too many things have to conspire to make the hand work.

For every situation, you want to determine your "conspiracy number," where you back down if that number of items has to conspire together. A conspiracy number of "three" is enough for me to back down in most things.

F) BE THE BANK.

I was once in Atlantic City and I was playing at a table with one of the best players I knew, Joe.

Another guy at the table needed chips and Joe said, "I'll sell you some of my chips." So the guy handed over money and Joe sold him some of his chips (an activity that is illegal in Atlantic City but it was 4 a.m. and nobody cared).

I asked Joe later why he did that. Joe said, "Always be the bank. If you're the source of everything at the table, then it makes it harder for them to bet against you."

This is a weird version of "give and you shall receive," but it works.

In September 1999, one year to the day after I started playing every day, I stopped.

I started another company instead and lost millions at it.

Perhaps then I realized that all of life is a game of high stakes poker. And on every hand you risk losing everything you've ever worked hard for.

Or maybe the final thing I learned is that it's all just a game. And eventually you can just stop playing. A first kiss is better than winning any hand.

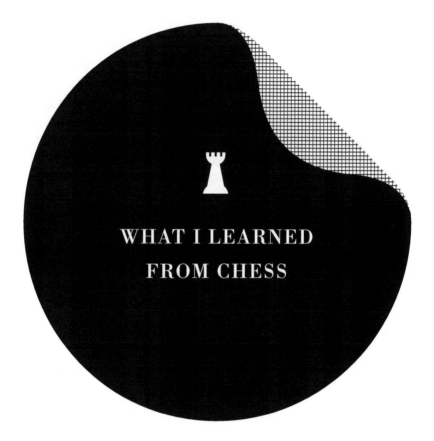

WHAT I LEARNED
FROM CHESS

C hess got me a girlfriend, it got me into college, it got me into graduate school, it got me my first job, it helped me raise money, it helped me sell my company, and it's opened doors that previously seemed locked to everyone around me.

But all of that is superficial. Where it really helped me, where any activity that you devote your heart to for years at a time helps you, is the following:

A) HOW TO LEARN

Many people play chess for years and never get better. I have one friend I see about once every five years. He loves chess but has never once studied the game.

He still plays the same moves. Makes the same mistakes. All of that time spent on something he loves and he is unable to improve.

How come? Hasn't he put in his 10,000 hours?

It's not about 10,000 hours. It's about 10,000 hours where you practice with intent.

You have to get a teacher. You have to study the history (play over the games played by all the great players since the 1800s through yesterday).

You have to study books on how to play the opening in chess. The middle game, (study books on tactics and positional strategy) and the end game (study books with problem after problem on how to play when there are few pieces on board).

You have to play and be willing to lose in order to learn more.

This is the same as anything. You get better at sales and management from studying from the best, reading and re-reading thousands of examples, and understanding the subtleties in the history of what you love.

B) HOW TO LOSE

When I first started to play, I improved my skill very quickly, but not my psychology.

I wanted to think I was a talented genius. I wasn't.

Talent is a spark that lights the fire. But the fire needs constant fuel to get bigger.

Maybe I had a tiny bit of talent, like most of us do. But I wasn't anything special.

I started playing at 17, which is very late for chess players to start playing. But within a year I was the strongest high school player in my state.

But along the way I played a match with my high school team. I lost. It was right after I had started taking lessons from one of the strongest grandmasters in the country.

It killed me to lose. What was the point? What was the point of my life? I had wrapped my personality up so much into chess that it was the only thing important to me.

I threw all the pieces on the floor and walked out. Everyone was laughing. I didn't come back to school for several days.

A few months later I was playing my father. Here I was, 17 years old, a grown man (almost), and when my father beat me I would start crying and yelling at him.

Another time, I was 18, and I was representing New Jersey in the U.S. High School Championship. I won my first game but lost my second game. I trashed my hotel room like I was some kind of rock star and I was so upset my grandparents had to drive down and pick me up. I dropped out of the tournament.

I would have nightmares when I lost. The game being played over and over again in my head. I was at expert level and not quite master.

Finally, I started to care more about getting better than about winning. I started to study my losses. I would take my losses to my instructor and we would go over them.

And that's how I went from expert-level to master-level.

I still don't like to lose. I hate it. It's the worst feeling. But I never let a good loss go to waste. The only way to learn is to study something you never knew before.

Losses are the maps that point you to what you never knew before.

C) HOW TO PLAY

I used to shake before every tournament. I was so nervous I always felt sick.

And sometimes in the middle of the game, it would look like I was on the verge of losing.

At first, if I was on the verge of losing, I would lose. It was like being stuck in the tractor beam of the Death Star. The loss would reel me in and all I could do was watch the mutilation of the pieces right in front of me.

But then I switched mindsets. If I realized I was losing, it almost became better for me. I would start to think, "OK, now the game begins. I have to get tricky."

I would spend more time at the board. I would focus. I would look down every variation.

There's a book called *Think Like a Grandmaster* by Alexander Kotov. He would suggest that before looking down any variations deeply, just look at all the "candidate moves" in front of you and then one by one start looking down them.

I would come up with more candidate moves. More ways to make things look confusing. More ways to scare my opponent into tripping up.

I became a better player by learning how to be mischievous when I was down. By learning how to kill when my opponent thought the hunt was already over.

By learning how not to give up when all hope was lost.

D) HOW TO CONTROL MY PARANOIA

Chess is about being paranoid.

When your opponent makes a move, he's not your friend. He's your predator. He wants to kill you.

So you look at every possibility. How is he trying to kill you? What is your worst-case scenario?

Much later, when I was managing money for people, I was always worried about what the worst scenarios could be. When I went out on dates I was also worried about the worst-case scenarios.

I was too paranoid. I was thinking too much that everyone was a predator.

It's true that everyone is self-interested. This is how people survive. But I learned to hone it in real life. 'OK, here's where I should paranoid. And here's where I should relax. But occasionally, here's where I should trigger someone else to be paranoid.'

And the good thing is chess taught me how to do that.

E) ADULTS

For the first time ever, I had friends who were not my age. I had friends of all ages and races and economic backgrounds.

One language united us, which was the language of chess. Even when I was much older, I could be friends with 15-year-olds because we would play chess and analyze the games together.

Or, one time I was in Buenos Aires, at the world famous chess club where Fischer beat Petrosian, where Alekhine beat Capablanca.

I don't speak Spanish and the guys running the club didn't speak

English. But the friend I was with told them my rating, and then ushered me right in.

I played games against the Argentinian junior champion, who was there, and we got the full tour the historical place.

Ever since I was a kid, I would go to Washington Square Park at the southwest corner, where the chess players have played for 60 years.

When I was younger it was mostly drug dealers and prostitutes hanging out there. But there were also chess players and backgammon players and Scrabble players (Scrabble more in the northwest corner).

Ultimately I crossed many barriers that a "civilian" life would not have allowed me to cross. Perhaps this is the thing I am most grateful for.

It's not just chess. If you get good at anything you get to speak a language that supersedes all other barriers, that builds a bridge directly into the hearts of others who share the same love.

F) HOW TO TAKE ADVANTAGE

Everyone thinks chess players are smart. It's a cultural myth.

It's not really true. There are smart ones and some that are very stupid.

But because of the myth around chess and IQ, I have been able to maneuver.

When I applied to college, my grades were very poor. But my

interviewer was a low-ranking chess player. So I helped him analyze some games for the entire hour of the interview. I then got into college.

When I applied to graduate school, every place rejected me except the one school that was working on the world's best chess computer. Guess who my office mate became?

When I applied for a job, all of my interviews went badly. I didn't know the answers to anything. I went outside in my hot, stuffy suit that didn't fit and called my girlfriend.

"Looks like I'm not good enough for New York."

I then went to play in the park right next door where tables were set up.

I beat the first person I played, a strong master. When I was done, I looked up and my boss's boss's boss was watching (if I got the job he would have that power over me). It turns out he was a player.

"I never saw anyone beat Ylon before," he said.

And we took an hour long walk around the park talking chess and Internet and TV and everything.

I got the job.

Then, 20 years later almost to the day, Ylon Schwartz, the guy I played in the park that day, came onto my podcast and we discussed poker, of which he is now a champion.

Chess had meant everything to me. I love it. I'm not the best at it. I'm just good enough to be better than most.

But you can have these results with anything you love. When you love something, instant community builds around you to protect you. You become something much bigger than yourself.

It turns out that evolution is not about individual selection. We only survive as well as we function in terms of a group. When we are a strong part of a group, when we help the group, and when we use the group's resources to become better as individuals, then we survive and even thrive.

For me, chess, business, writing, has done that.

I no longer throw pieces at the people who beat me. I no longer even really study the game. I've chosen to focus more on writing and other things.

But it's inside of me and will be forever.

*   *   *

WHAT TO DO RIGHT NOW

* *Find your Plus.*
* *Find your Equal.*
* *Find your Minus.*

I never once made a big change in my life without the above three.

Along with that, I do the check every day:

Did I improve 1% physically, emotionally, creatively, spiritually?

If you can check those four boxes by the end of the day, that's the best predictor that tomorrow will be a good day.

I've had over 15 "careers." I put it in quotes because I always thought a career would last a lifetime.

It hasn't for me. I seem to be always reinventing. I get curious about a new field and I want to learn everything I can.

Then I get excited about a new field, learn everything there. Then sometimes I combine the fields. Sometimes I make money. Sometimes I move on. Sometimes I explore more.

Who knows?

Once this book is published (which means: before you are reading it) I am going to begin the path of reinvention again. Life seems longer, the more chapters of it I can experience.

We can live life like today is our last—what worthwhile thing will we do today?

Or we can live life like we are going to live forever. So we have all the time in the world to learn and live all the things we love.

This is the path I want to take. Not the path we're programmed from birth to take. Nor the path that is unique and lonely.

I want to take the path of reinvention. This, to me, is how we carve out our particular definition of success, how we live a life with as few regrets as possible, and how we succeed using the code of the amateur.

In the past six years I've written maybe 2,000 articles and done hundreds of interviews with peak performers in every area of life.

Some of that knowledge I've tried to distill into this book. Some of it has infected my way of life, changing me completely over and over.

Reinvention is never over. Today is the first day.

APPENDIX

This last section is reprinted from the *Choose Yourself Guide to Wealth*. It's critically important for reinvention.

....

THE GUIDE TO REINVENTING YOURSELF

A. **REINVENTION NEVER STOPS.**

Every day you reinvent yourself. You're always in motion. But you decide every day: forward or backward.

B. **YOU START FROM SCRATCH.**

Every label you claim you have from before is just vanity. You were a doctor? You were Ivy League? You had millions? You had a family? Nobody cares. You lost everything. You're a zero. Don't try to say you're anything else.

C. **YOU NEED A MENTOR.**

Else, you'll sink to the bottom. Someone has to show you how to move and breathe. But don't worry about finding a mentor (see below).

D. **THREE TYPES OF MENTORS**

1. **DIRECT.** Someone who is in front of you who will show you how they did it. What is "it"? Wait. By the way, mentors aren't like that old Japanese guy in "The Karate Kid." Ultimately most mentors will hate you.

2. **INDIRECT.** Books. You can outsource 90 percent of mentorship to books and other materials. 200-500 books equals one good mentor. People ask me, "What is a good book to read?" I never know the answer. There are 200-500 good books to read. I would throw in inspirational books. Whatever are your beliefs, underline them through reading every day.

3. **EVERYTHING IS A MENTOR.** If you are a zero, and have passion for reinvention, then everything you look at will be a metaphor for what you want to do. The tree you see, with roots you don't, with underground water that feeds it, is a metaphor for computer programming if you connect the dots. And everything you look at, you will connect the dots.

E. **DON'T WORRY IF YOU DON'T HAVE PASSION FOR ANYTHING.**

You have passion for your health. Start there. Take baby steps. You don't need a passion to succeed. Do what you do with love and success is a natural symptom.

F. **TIME IT TAKES TO REINVENT YOURSELF: FIVE YEARS.**

Here's a description of the five years:

1. *Year One:* you're flailing and reading everything and just starting to DO.

2. *Year Two:* you know who you need to talk to and network with. You're Doing every day. You finally know what the monopoly board looks like in your new endeavors.

3. *Year Three:* you're good enough to start making money. It might not be a living yet.

4. *Year Four:* you're making a good living

5. *Year Five:* you're making wealth

Sometimes I get frustrated in years 1-4. I say, "why isn't it happening yet?" and I punch the floor and hurt my hand and throw a coconut on the floor in a weird ritual. That's okay. Just keep going. Or stop and pick a new field. It doesn't matter. Eventually you're dead and then it's hard to reinvent yourself.

G. **IF YOU DO THIS FASTER OR SLOWER THEN YOU ARE DOING SOMETHING WRONG.**

Google is a good example.

H. **IT'S NOT ABOUT THE MONEY. BUT MONEY IS A DECENT MEASURING STICK.**

When people say "it's not about the money" they should make sure they have a different measuring stick.

"What about just doing what you love?" There will be many days when you don't love what you are doing. If you are doing it just for love then it will take much much longer than five years.

Happiness is just a positive perception from our brain. Some days you will be unhappy. Our brain is a tool we use. It's not who we are.

I. **WHEN CAN YOU SAY, "I DO X!" WHERE X IS YOUR NEW CAREER?**

Today.

J.   WHEN CAN I START DOING X?

Today. If you want to paint, then buy a canvas and paints today, start buying 500 books one at a time, and start painting. If you want to write do these three things:

- Read

- Write

- Take your favorite author and type your favorite story of his word for word. Wonder to yourself why he wrote each word. He's your mentor today.

If you want to start a business, start spec-ing out the idea for your business. Reinvention starts today. Every day.

K.   HOW DO I MAKE MONEY?

By year three you've put in 5,000-7,000 hours. That's good enough to be in the top 200-300 in the world in anything. The top 200 in almost any field makes a living.

By year three you will know how to make money. By year four you will scale that up and make a living. Some people stop at year four.

L.   BY YEAR FIVE YOU'RE IN THE TOP 30-50 SO YOU CAN MAKE WEALTH.

M.   WHAT IS "IT"? HOW DO I KNOW WHAT I SHOULD DO?

Whatever area you feel like reading 500 books about. Go to the bookstore and find it. If you get bored three months later go back to the bookstore.

It's okay to get disillusioned. That's what failure is about. Success is better than failure but the biggest lessons are found in failure.

Very important: There's no rush. You will reinvent yourself many times in an interesting life. You will fail to reinvent many times. That's fun also.

Many reinventions make your life a book of stories instead of a textbook.

Some people want the story of their life to be a textbook. For better or worse, mine is a book of stories.

That's why reinvention happens every day.

N.   THE CHOICES YOU MAKE TODAY WILL BE IN YOUR BIOGRAPHY TOMORROW.

Make interesting choices and you will have an interesting biography.

N1.   THE CHOICES YOU MAKE TODAY WILL BE IN YOUR BIOGRAPHY
Tomorrow.

O.   WHAT IF I LIKE SOMETHING OBSCURE? LIKE BIBLICAL ARCHAEOLOGY OR 11TH-CENTURY WARFARE?

Repeat all of the steps above, and then in year five you will make wealth. We have no idea how. Don't look to find the end of the road when you are still at the very first step.

P. WHAT IF MY FAMILY WANTS ME TO BE AN AC-COUNTANT?

How many years of your life did you promise your family? Ten years? Your whole life? Then wait until the next life. The good thing is: you get to choose.

Choose freedom over family. Freedom over preconceptions. Freedom over government. Freedom over people-pleasing. Then you will be pleased.

Q. MY MENTOR WANTS ME TO DO IT HIS WAY.

That's fine. Learn HIS way. Then do it YOUR way. With respect. Hopefully nobody has a gun to your head. Then you have to do it their way until the gun is put down.

R. MY SPOUSE IS WORRIED ABOUT WHO WILL SUPPORT/TAKE CARE OF KIDS?

Then after you work 16 hours a day, seven days a week being a janitor, use your spare time to reinvent.

Someone who is reinventing ALWAYS has spare time. Part of reinvention is collecting little bits and pieces of time and re-carving them the way you want them to be.

S. WHAT IF MY FRIENDS THINK I'M CRAZY?

What friends?

T. WHAT IF I WANT TO BE AN ASTRONAUT?

That's not a reinvention. That's a specific job. If you like "outer space" there are many careers. Richard Branson wanted to be an astronaut and started Virgin Galactic.

U. WHAT IF I LIKE TO GO OUT DRINKING AND PARTYING?

Read this post again in a year.

V. WHAT IF I'M BUSY CHEATING ON MY HUSBAND OR WIFE OR BETRAYING A PARTNER?

Read this post again in two or three years when you are broke and jobless and nobody likes you.

W. WHAT IF I HAVE NO SKILLS AT ALL?

Read "B" again.

X. WHAT IF I HAVE NO DEGREE OR I HAVE A USELESS DEGREE?

Read "B" again.

Y. WHAT IF I HAVE TO FOCUS ON PAYING DOWN MY DEBT AND MORTGAGE?

Read "R" again.

Z. HOW COME I ALWAYS FEEL LIKE I'M ON THE OUTSIDE LOOKING IN?

Albert Einstein was on the outside looking in. Nobody in the establishment would even hire him.

Everyone feels like a fraud at some point. The highest form of creativity is born out of skepticism.

AA. I CAN'T READ 500 BOOKS. WHAT ONE BOOK SHOULD I READ FOR INSPIRATION?

Give up.

BB. WHAT IF I'M TOO SICK TO REINVENT?

Reinvention will boost every healthy chemical in your body: serotonin, dopamine, oxytocin. Keep moving forward and you might not get healthy but you will get healthier. Don't use health as an excuse.

Finally, reinvent your health first. Sleep more hours. Eat better. Exercise. These are key steps to reinvention.

CC. WHAT IF MY LAST PARTNER SCREWED ME AND I'M STILL SUING HIM?

Stop litigating and never think about him again. Half the problem was you, not him.

DD. WHAT IF I'M GOING TO JAIL?

Perfect. Reread "B." Read a lot of books in jail.

EE. WHAT IF I'M SHY?

Make your weaknesses your strengths. Introverts listen better, focus better, and have ways of being more endearing.

FF. WHAT IF I CAN'T WAIT FIVE YEARS?

If you plan on being alive in five years then you might as well start today.

GG. HOW SHOULD I NETWORK?

- Make concentric circles. You're at the middle.
- The next circle is friends and family.
- The next circle is online communities.
- The circle after that is meetups and coffees.

- The circle after that is conferences and thought leaders.
- The circle after that is mentors.
- The circle after that is customers and wealth-creators.
- Start making your way through the circles.

HH. WHAT HAPPENS WHEN I HAVE EGO ABOUT WHAT I DO?

In 6-12 months you'll be back at "B."

II. WHAT IF I'M PASSIONATE ABOUT TWO THINGS? WHAT IF I CAN'T DECIDE?

Combine them and you'll be the best in the world at the combination.

JJ. WHAT IF I'M SO EXCITED I WANT TO TEACH WHAT I'M LEARNING?

Start teaching on YouTube. Start with an audience of one and see if it builds up.

KK. WHAT IF I WANT TO MAKE MONEY WHILE I SLEEP?

In year four, start outsourcing what you do.

LL. HOW DO I MEET MENTORS AND THOUGHT LEADERS?

Once you have enough knowledge (after 100-200 books), write down 10 ideas for 20 different potential mentors.

None of them will respond. Write down 10 more ideas for 20 new mentors. Repeat every week.

Put together a newsletter for everyone who doesn't respond. Keep repeating until someone responds. Blog about your learning efforts. Build community around you being an expert.

MM.   **WHAT IF I CAN'T COME UP WITH IDEAS?**

Then keep practicing coming up with ideas. The idea muscle atrophies. You have to build it up.

It's hard for me to touch my toes if I haven't been doing it every day. I have to do it every day for a while before I can easily touch my toes. Don't expect to come up with good ideas on day one.

NN.   **WHAT ELSE SHOULD I READ?**

AFTER books, read websites, forums, magazines. But most of that is garbage.

OO.   **WHAT IF I DO EVERYTHING YOU SAY BUT IT STILL DOESN'T SEEM LIKE IT'S WORKING?**

It will work. Just wait. Keep reinventing every day.

Don't try and find the end of the road. You can't see it in the fog. But you can see the next step and you *do* know that if you take that next step eventually you get to the end of the road.

PP.   **WHAT IF I GET DEPRESSED?**

Sit in silence for one hour a day. You need to get back to your core.

If you think this sounds stupid then don't do it. Stay depressed.

QQ. WHAT IF I DON'T HAVE TIME TO SIT IN SILENCE?

Then sit in silence for two hours a day. This is not meditation. This is just sitting.

RR. WHAT IF I GET SCARED?

Sleep 8-9 hours a day and never gossip. Sleep is the No. 1 key to successful health. It's not the only key. It's just No. 1. Some people write to me and say, "I only need four hours of sleep" or "in my country sleeping means laziness." Well, those people will fail and die young.

What about gossip? The brain biologically wants to have 150 friends. Then when you are with one of your friends you can gossip about any of the other 150. If you don't have 150 friends then the brain wants to read gossip magazines until it thinks it has 150 friends.

Don't be as stupid as your brain.

SS. WHAT IF I KEEP FEELING LIKE NOTHING EVER WORKS OUT FOR ME?

Spend 10 minutes a day practicing gratitude. Don't suppress the fear. Notice the anger.

But also allow yourself to be grateful for the things you do have. Anger is never inspirational but gratitude is. Gratitude is the bridge between your world and the parallel universe where all creative ideas live.

TT. WHAT IF I HAVE TO DEAL WITH PERSONAL BULLSHIT ALL THE TIME?

Find new people to be around.

Someone who is reinventing herself will constantly find people to try and bring her down. The brain is scared of reinvention because it might not be safe.

Biologically, the brain wants you to be safe and reinvention is a risk. So it will throw people in your path who will try to stop you.

Learn how to say "no."

UU. **WHAT IF I'M HAPPY AT MY CUBICLE JOB?**

Good luck.

VV. **WHY SHOULD I TRUST YOU – YOU'VE FAILED SO MANY TIMES?**

Don't trust me.

WW. **WILL YOU BE MY MENTOR?**

You've just read this book.

Reinvent
YOURSELF

* ✦ *

JAMES ALTUCHER

COPYRIGHT © JAMES ALTUCHER, 2016. ALL RIGHTS RESERVED.

All rights reserved. No part of this publication may be reproduced, stored in or introduced into a retrieval system, or transmitted, in any form or by any means (electronically, mechanically, via photocopying, recording or otherwise), without the prior written permission of both the copyright owner and the publisher of this book. The scanning, uploading, and distribution of this book via the Internet or via any other means without the permission of the publisher is illegal and punishable by law.

Printed in the United States of America.

CATALOG:
ALTUCHER, JAMES
 Reinvent Yourself / James Altucher
p. cm.

First Edition
Interior designed by: Erin Tyler

CHOOSE YOURSELF
MEDIA LLC.

45980275R00227

Made in the USA
San Bernardino, CA
22 February 2017